REVERENCE

Reverence

Echoes of Healing & Gratitude

Judy Stella

ALEgRÍA

PUBLISHING

Book Design by Diane Castañeda
Book Cover Image by Monica Martin
Edited by Samantha M. Ryan

Disclaimer: Portions of this book are works on nonfiction. Certain names and identifying details have been changed to protect the privacy of individuals.

The information in this book is provided for informational purposes only and should not be used to replace the specialized training and professional judgement of a health care or mental health care professional.

Neither the author nor the publisher can be held responsible for the use of the information provided within this book. Please, always consult a trained professional before making any decisions regarding treatment of yourself or others.

ISBN: 9798988174691

Published by Alegria Publishing

"You see things; and you say, 'Why?'
But I dream things that never were;
and I say, 'Why not?'"

-George Bernard Shaw

Dedication

This book is dedicated to all those who courageously open its pages, seeking solace and wisdom for their healing journey. May the stories within illuminate the transformative power of reverence, inspiring a profound appreciation for the beauty and resilience within each one of us. May you recognize your own strength, your own worth, and the boundless potential that lies within your soul.

Foreword by Dr. Farhat Chaudhry

As I embark upon the profound privilege of introducing this poignant memoir, I envision this beautiful, happy little five-year-old in her pink polka dotted skirt coming to life off the pages in the most playful way childhood should be experienced. As I go deeper into her world, her soul carries the heaviness that no child should have to bear. Her words paint a vivid portrait of how her world was shrouded in the darkness of pain inflicted by those she loved, those entrusted to protect them from the evils of society and not be the source of the torment they suffer.

It is within these pages that you will find the transformation of this beautiful yet terrified little girl into the courageous voice of Judy, a daughter, a sister, a wife, a friend and, most importantly, a mother, bravely recounting her journey through the shadows of childhood marked by unspeakable abuse that she is finally able to give voice to. The hurdles she faced were not merely external but deeply entrenched within her psyche, woven into the fabric of her identity. This is not only a narrative of a survivor of abuse, but a testament of a woman not willing to be shackled by the echoes of her past.

In the safety of our therapeutic space, Judy began the journey of unraveling the tangled threads of her past. Each session was a delicate balance of holding space for her pain and gently guiding her towards the path of healing. As Judy began to lay bare her scars of childhood, the recognition that her innocence was betrayed and trust shattered, came with the power of a dam breaking in a storm. She realized how much she had been questioning her own worth, and coming to the haunting realization of how the drowning in a sea of self-doubt, guilt, and shame, entirety of her life had been so deeply affected by her past.

As I observed her throughout the years, Judy mustered up the courage to face each of the challenges that she has recollected between the pages that are about to unfold before you. I saw her fight to reclaim herself and not let the past, the abuse, or the mistrust dictate her life. My role was not to fix her pain or erase her scars, but to bear witness to her journey, provide a safe haven in a storm of turmoil, and help her see who she truly was—and is—from within. The light of hope and the desire to be the best version of herself guided her every session. The word to best describe her path on this therapeutic journey is "resilient." As she faced her past, she wanted to grow, she wanted to change, she had a sense of resilience that refused to be extinguished by any challenges that her conscious and subconscious memories brought forth.

To rewrite her narrative, to reclaim her voice and her agency in a society that would not give her space to do so, Judy had to be vulnerable. But, to be vulnerable and bare her deepest wounds on pages for others to lay eyes on, meant risking everything to expose the raw, unfiltered truth of these experiences to the scrutiny of strangers—a very arduous task that took strength and resilience to do so. Judy had to put aside the fear of judgment, the possible dismissal of her pain by others, or even worse, the possibility of being blamed for the horrors she endured, in order to share her story in an effort to empower others.

This selfless act came with the price of being re-traumatized, which she prepared for and had expected as she delved more deeply into her life. She had to relive the scenes of her childhood, confront the demons that had haunted her for so long, and reopen old wounds. Judy once again, in writing this book, had to subject herself to the pain and anguish that she had fought so hard to bury long ago. She took on this challenge and endured this trial for the sake of giving voice to those that can connect with her story and come out stronger while on this journey with her. With each word written, she was determined to give voice to her pain, reclaim a piece of herself, showing others that it is possible to transform pain into power and vulnerability into strength. As the sessions went on, I witnessed Judy shed the layers of her trauma that bound her to the years of her past and emerge stronger and more resilient than ever before.

As Judy walked this courageous journey of writing her book, I saw her confront her vulnerabilities with an unwavering resolve, converting pain into power, and silence into strength. Through all the hurdles and difficulties, writing came so naturally to her, as she has the deepest desires to protect, nurture, and impart wisdom that she gained through her life experiences to others in an effort to lessen challenges that life may present their way. The interactive pages of her book speak to that imparting of knowledge. As you read her words and think of your life journey through a questioning lens, she enables you to give yourself permission to let the past be acknowledged and processed.

Within these pages lies not only the story of a strong, resilient woman shuffling through her childhood but of a daughter with the daunting task of reconciling the fractured pieces of her relationship with her mother, the scars of their past threatening to tear them apart. Nonetheless this daughter navigated the tumultuous waters with grace, humility, and a heart full of forgiveness.

For her father, she felt an unwavering sense of compassion and determination to make him a part of her present from beyond. As the love grew so complex, even she was perplexed at how she forged such strong and authentic familial connections with a man she had only faded memories of.

As a sister, she stood tall as the pillar of strength, offering solace and sanctuary in the midst of shared pain. With each act of kindness and understanding, she breathed a new life into the sibling bond, transforming trauma into a source of solidarity and unity to nurture the sibling relationship.

As a wife, she built a loving relationship of unwavering honesty and vulnerability. Each of them laying aside their deepest fears and insecurities and partnering together through their shared love and commitment to their relationship and to their family to live life together.

As a friend, she became a source of inspiration for those lucky enough to be called her friends. Being of a compassionate heart and unwavering empathy, she offered a listening ear, a shoulder to lean on as she guided them while also bearing her own struggles with grace and wisdom.

As a mother, she confronted the profound responsibility of breaking the cycle of abuse with boundless love in a home filled with warmth, compassion, safety, and unconditional acceptance, empowering her children to embrace their own journeys with courage, humility, and grace. Through her laughter, tears, words and actions, she imparted so many invaluable lessons of compassion, resilience, and self-love to her two beautiful children that are the coolness of her eyes and the serene breeze of her every breath.

In every role she inhabits, Judy embodies the true essence of courage—a courage born not of bravado or strength, but of vulnerability and resilience. Through sharing her personal journey of healing and the use of her words and actions, she has transformed her pain into empowerment, her silence into strength, and her trauma into triumph.

The future is sure to be fraught with its new challenges, but I have no doubt that Judy will continue to grow and shine brightly, luminating the path for others who may find themselves navigating similar shadows.

With honor, love, and unwavering admiration,

Dr. Farhat Bari Chaudhry,
Doctor of Psychology,
Licensed Marriage and Family Therapist,
in the State of California

Preface

From the earliest days of my childhood, books were my sanctuary. Within their silent pages, I found comfort, escape, and glimpses of my own struggles and dreams. I never realized then that sharing my own story would become an inevitable part of my journey.

For years, I carried the weight of guilt and shame, believing it was mine to bear forever. Yet life, in its mysterious way, led me towards healing, revealing unexpected paths. Through various forms of expression, I discovered not just liberation, but also a deep reverence for the path I've walked.

As I write these words now, I do so with the hope that they may reach those who need them most. To you, dear reader, I offer these chapters of my life not as tales of victory or defeat, but as a beacon of shared humanity, the transformative power of healing within the community, and what I like to refer to as earthly angels.

May the stories within these pages touch your heart, offering insights and reflections to guide you on your own journey of healing and self-discovery. As you immerse yourself in these words, may you find the strength to shape your destiny, to pursue your dreams with unwavering resolve, and to treasure the moments that give life its true meaning.

ONE

"Judy, ¡vamos! Date prisa, le voy a preguntar al señor si la casa está lista para alquilar," my mother's urgent voice pierced the air, snapping me out of my childish musings. With a quick shake of my head, I refocused my attention and hastened to keep up with her determined strides. Little did I know that this hurried moment would mark the beginning of my life story—a narrative teeming with untold tales, waiting to be shared with the world.

Lennox, California—affectionately known as "Little TJ" by those who cherish its distinct community and vibrant culture—is a town often shrouded in obscurity, overshadowed by the bustling cities of Hawthorne and Inglewood. A hidden gem nestled just a stone's throw away from the magnificence of LAX Airport.

In our neighborhood, I found myself immersed in a diverse Latin community. Latin grocery stores dotted the streets, bustling with activity. The air was alive with the rhythmic beats of cumbias, rancheras, and the romantic melodies of Los Bukis. Life seemed to sway to the rhythm of ranchera music, accompanied by the cheerful jingles of paleta carts selling paletas de chicle y limon. The delicious smell of homemade tamales drifted through the streets, carrying stories of our shared experiences, communal hardships, and cultural traditions. It was a place where neighbors were more than just acquaintances—they were like family.

My earliest memory of Lennox brings me back to the days just before my fifth birthday. Dressed in a twirling pink skirt adorned with playful black polka dots and black shiny shoes accentuated by dainty ribbons, I scurried to keep pace with my mother's sense of urgency.

Standing tall before us was a beautiful blue two-story house, set amidst a tranquil scene. The gentle sway of green trees framed the house like protective sentinels, while a long cement pathway stretched out before us, showing us the way to the entrance. It was as though the pathway itself was leading us towards the house, guiding our approach with its steady presence. Along its edges, patches of earth adorned with delicate white flowers adding an extra touch of charm to the serene surroundings.

As I strolled down the street, a melodious tune caught my ear, guiding my gaze across the busy street to the quaint Arreola's grocery store. Adorning its walls stood a vibrant mural of the Virgen de Guadalupe, her serene presence seemingly overseeing the spirited neighborhood. The colors of the mural were rich and captivating, immediately drawing me into its beauty. The Virgin Mary, depicted in all her glory, served as a symbol of hope and faith for many residents in the community. Her presence soon became a source of comfort, a beacon of light in my life. For those who lived there, she was a constant reminder of the power of faith and the strength derived from believing in something greater than oneself. Her image adorned the walls of homes and businesses alike, a magnificent sight that inspired reverence and devotion in all who beheld it and prayed for the miracles of each passing day.

But before I could fully immerse myself in the scene, my mother's commanding voice interrupted my reverie, reminding me not to get distracted. With a firm tone, she directed my gaze towards the majestic blue house standing tall before us. As I craned my neck to take in its grandeur, my young mind struggled to comprehend the significance of this moment.

Unbeknownst to me, this house would become the cornerstone of my life—a dwelling that witnessed my triumphs, struggles, and the untold chapters that would unfold within its walls, forever changing the course of my existence.

In the heart of Lennox lies a treasure trove of memories, tucked away in its humble surroundings. Among these cherished moments is the story of lazy afternoons spent at the neighborhood park, where time seemed to slow down, allowing family bonds to flourish. The park, a sanctuary of joy and innocence, witnessed our laughter echoing through the air as we embarked on adventures fueled by childhood imagination.

With my siblings by my side, our mother would treat us to simple joys, like delicious raspados from a colorful cart. We would take turns soaring through the sky on creaky swings and conquer the towering rocket ship, casting ourselves into the cosmos of limitless possibilities.

Amid the joy and playful moments, there's one memory that shines brightly, a memory that captures my mother's love and care perfectly. As the sun reached its peak, painting the park with a golden glow, my mother would unveil a lunch bag packed with my favorite fruits. Inside, nestled among the folds, were juicy mangos, sweet oranges, slices of pepino with a zesty lime drizzle, and a sprinkle of Pico de Gallo chili powder. Those moments in the park, with the tantalizing aroma of fruits mingling with the laughter of my siblings, remain etched in my heart. They show how deeply my mother loved us and how she turned even the simplest moments into something magical—a reminder of the simple yet profound way my mother showed her love.

As I reflect on my childhood, I am struck by the profound influence it wielded in shaping the person I am today. Those humble beginnings served as the foundation for the extraordinary journey that awaited me, a journey woven intricately with the essence of Lennox. In this town, I weathered my most agonizing trials, tasted the sweetness of love, and confronted some of life's toughest decisions. It was within the vibrant tapestry of Lennox that my story found its roots—a place I proudly proclaim as my first home, a testament to the resilience of the human spirit and the enduring power of community.

Judy Stella

TWO

We moved into our new house shortly after that initial visit, but the reality of our new home was far from what I had envisioned. Instead of a sprawling two-story house, we found ourselves settling into a single bedroom with a modest kitchenette attached to the side. The short-lived vision of living in a two-story home quickly faded, replaced by the humbleness of our new home.

Our belongings were sparse, a testament to the simplicity of our lives. There was one main piece of furniture: a worn and weathered brown loveseat that would serve as my bed. I would curl up beneath my blanket, finding solace in its familiar embrace, while my mother slept beside me on the floor. We had our clothes and a small basket that held my cherished toys, but beyond that, our possessions were minimal.

The realization soon dawned on me that we would be sharing the bathroom and shower with the other occupants of the house. Our room, nestled on the second floor, was accompanied by three other bedrooms occupied by fellow tenants. These individuals, strangers, who would become my new neighbors and unknowingly play a significant role in our lives.

As I observed our surroundings, it became clear that this new living arrangement was about more than just sharing a roof. It was a lesson in humility, resilience, and finding strength in unexpected places. In the midst of uncertainty, a newfound sense of community emerged. These neighbors, once strangers, became pillars of support and empathy. Within the walls of our shared residence, bonds were forged, and acts of kindness became the currency of our everyday lives.

It was in our shared existence that I discovered that sometimes the truest forms of support and compassion can emerge from the unlikeliest of places. Our little bedroom in that house, despite its humble appearance, was a testament to the resilience and fortitude that resided within us. It became a space where hope thrived, where we found solace in our shared experiences, and where the seeds of gratitude for our newfound community were sown. But this is just the beginning. As you read on, you'll see how our simple room shaped my early life in ways you wouldn't expect.

THREE

Our new home was a place filled with magic waiting to happen, where every corner held the promise of cherished memories. One such moment stands out vividly in my mind. It was right after we had settled in; our furniture was sparse, but our hearts were full of excitement.

I remember sitting on the only piece of furniture we owned with my mother beside me, holding a book she had borrowed from my school. It was a story that would soon become my favorite— *Caperucita Roja* (Little Red Riding Hood). My mom would indulge me, reading the tale repeatedly, each time with as much enthusiasm as the last.

I loved watching her face light up as she animatedly brought the characters to life. But my favorite part was when Little Red Riding Hood reached her grandmother's house, only to find the big bad wolf pretending to be her. That's when the magic truly began.

"Grandma, why do you have such big eyes?" I'd ask, and my mom would widen her eyes, altering her voice to match the character.

"So that I can see you better," she'd reply, sending shivers of excitement down my spine.

Then came the iconic question.

"Grandma, what big teeth you have!"

Without missing a beat, my mother would once again transform, her voice dropping low.

"It's so that I can eat you better," she'd growl playfully, opening her arms wide as if ready to pounce.

Each time, I'd play along, pretending to escape the clutches of the wolf. And without fail, it always ended in a warm embrace, both of us laughing until tears welled up in our eyes.

In that simple exchange, amidst the laughter and the joy, we built a bond that would endure a lifetime. Those moments of storytelling and make-believe became the foundation of our relationship, filling our home with love and laughter. And to this day, it remains one of my most cherished memories with my mother, held closely to my heart.

FOUR

In our new home, I encountered my first neighbor, María. She and her husband occupied the room adjacent to ours, and it didn't take long for her and my mother to strike up a close friendship, having met at work. María's vivacious spirit was infectious, always ready with a playful joke, and her laughter would echo through the walls at all times of the day. Even though I didn't always understand her humor, being around her made me feel comfortable.

María's friendship extended beyond mere pleasantries. On occasions when my mother had to be away, Maria would step in to take care of me while my mom had to work, offering me not only sustenance but also a comforting embrace. She became a source of stability during moments of uncertainty, offering me solace and protection.

One fateful afternoon, a frightening incident took place. I don't remember exactly how it all began, but I recall my mother's fury directed at me, her rage palpable as she advanced from the kitchen, wearing a stare that sent shivers down my spine. Harsh words spilled from her lips.

"Hija de la chingada, eres una pendeja" laced with venomous threats, "Te voy a poner una buena putiza, cabrona" and derogatory slurs that stung my tender soul. Terrified, I instinctively curled into a fetal position, hoping to make myself inconspicuous and shielded from her wrath.

As my mother's anger intensified, tears streamed down my face, mixing with my fear. In a trembling voice, barely heard, I whispered a desperate plea to myself, "I wish I could escape." I implored my mother not to hurt me, but her fury continued unabated, her words slicing through the air like sharpened blades, leaving me feeling utterly worthless.

Unable to endure the onslaught any longer, I sprinted toward Maria's door, my tiny fists pounding on it as I cried out her name.

"María, María, abre la puerta, pronto!"

Startled and bewildered by the urgency in my voice, she quickly opened the door, allowing me refuge in her modest home. Trembling, I sought safety under her dining table, a fortress shielding me from the chaos unfolding beyond its wooden legs.

My mother chased after me, her anger undeterred, but María stood resolute in the doorway, acting as a shield between us. She engaged my mother in a conversation that felt like an eternity, her voice a calming melody in stark contrast to the fear and tempest within me. In that single moment, María's unwavering presence offered me a glimpse of safety and respite from my mother's fury.

The aftermath of that encounter remains fragmented in my memory. I cannot recall how long I remained hidden beneath the table or the precise path I took when returning to our room. But one thing is forever etched in my heart: I will never forget María's kindness and her unwavering protection during my most vulnerable moment.

That day became an indescribable weight within me, a memory that lingered long after the storm had passed. It was a moment that exposed my fragility and engulfed me in fear, but it also revealed the profound significance of having someone by your side in times of turmoil. María went beyond being a neighbor; she became a guardian angel, demonstrating the unconditional love and support that can shield a vulnerable child from harm.

As a child, I may not have fully comprehended the complexity of the situation, but today I understand the profound impact of María's compassion and protection. Looking back now, I am immensely grateful for her presence in my life. In her embrace, I found solace, and through her kindness, I discovered the power of unwavering support and the resilience of the human spirit. María became more than our next door neighbor, she became my beacon of hope, reminding me that even in the darkest of times, there are those who will stand as guardians, ready to offer their love and protection.

FIVE

Don Paco, a resident who lived alongside his wife Ana in the room to the left of ours, was a person I could never forget. He embodied the same thoughtfulness and kindness that had become a defining characteristic of our new community. One afternoon, a moment unfolded that forever etched itself in my heart, illuminating the profound impact of even the smallest acts of love.

It was during a visit to their room that Ana extended an invitation for me to join them. With an eager nod, I accepted, brimming with anticipation. As I entered their humble place, the aroma of freshly baked pan dulce filled the air, instantly enticing my senses. My excitement grew, knowing that a sweet treat awaited me.

Taking a seat at their dining table, I noticed a solitary, rectangular piece of wood resting before me. Don Paco, with his warm smile, glanced over and caught my eye. To my delight, he reached out to his left, retrieving a canister of markers from the nearby cabinet. The mystery of the wooden canvas and his artistic intentions piqued my curiosity, and I adjusted my posture, trying to catch glimpses of his creative process.

With patience and precision, Don Paco began to draw on the wooden surface, intermittently requesting my input for color choices. Each moment felt like an eternity as I eagerly awaited the unveiling of his masterpiece. I strained to catch even the faintest hint of what was taking shape before my eyes.

After what felt like an eternity, Don Paco stood up, a radiant smile gracing his face.

"Ya está, ¿lista para ver lo que dibujé?" he asked, his voice filled with anticipation. I responded with an exuberant smile and an enthusiastic nod, unable to contain my excitement.

In a ceremonious display, Don Paco turned the wood piece toward me. At its center, my name, "Feliz Navidad, Judy," was beautifully inscribed. Surrounding the edges, vibrant images of birds, bells, and poinsettia flowers danced together in a symphony of color. Overwhelmed with joy, Don Paco extended his arms, placed the wooden creation in my hands, and spoke the words that would forever echo in my heart: "Es para ti; Feliz Navidad Judy".

Recalling this experience now, I am overcome with a surge of gratitude, a profound sense of appreciation for Don Paco's small but profound act of kindness. As a young child, to be seen and cherished, to have someone devote their time and creativity to craft something so unique and special was a moment that left a lasting mark on my soul.

That wooden masterpiece, bearing my name and the festive symbols of the holiday season, represented more than just a tangible gift. It was a symbol of love, a testament to the power of connection, and a reminder that even within the confines of our modest living space, beauty could flourish. Don Paco's artistic gesture served as a gentle reminder that amidst the challenges we faced, the love and compassion of those around us had the power to transcend boundaries, bringing light and joy into our lives.

Reflecting on that tender moment, I am grateful for the presence of Don Paco and Ana in our lives. They not only filled our days with laughter through shared meals but also granted me the gift of belonging, reminding us that within the tapestry of our shared existence, each thread is woven with care and purpose. Their genuine acts of kindness transformed our new home into a haven, a place where compassion and creativity coexisted, nurturing the seeds of hope, and emphasizing the importance of community.

SIX

As I regained consciousness, confusion clouded my mind as I tried to make sense of the unfamiliar surroundings. As I lay on the cold pavement, my mind struggled to comprehend the chaos surrounding me. The world seemed hazy, and my memories were fragments lost in the depths of unconsciousness.

Waking up to find myself sprawled in the middle of the street was terrifying, especially with my mother's anguished cries cutting through the confusion. As I glanced around, trying to make sense of the scene, the familiar sight of the wall mural depicting La Virgencita served as a faint anchor, quickly helping me gain consciousness and noticing my surroundings amid the chaos and loud noises. The flashing lights of fire trucks and ambulances added an eerie glow to the neighborhood I called home.

Paramedics hurried around me, their voices muffled and distant. I could hear their urgent questions, but I couldn't comprehend them, let alone respond. Moments later, they gently lifted me onto a gurney and transported me into the waiting ambulance. My mother, her face etched with worry, was allowed to accompany me.

As time passed, fragments of the incident were pieced together, painting a grim picture of what had occurred that night. It appeared that in my excitement to visit my friend Lucia, who lived just across the street from me; I had rushed down the stairs without caution. I remember seeing my neighbor, "El Cubano" and saying hello as he tipped his hat down with a smile. However, the events following my descent remained a blur.

Oblivious to the lurking dangers, I dashed across the street only to be struck by a car driven by a woman who failed to see me. The impact sent me sprawling beneath the vehicle, dragged mercilessly for several feet.

In a stroke of fortune, my neighbor emerged as an unlikely hero. Witnessing the accident, he sprinted towards the street, frantically waving his arms and yelling for the driver to stop. His quick thinking and selflessness ultimately saved my life.

People spoke of the "what ifs" that haunted the aftermath. If the driver hadn't been alerted by my neighbor's intervention, if she had continued driving, I might not have survived that night. The gravity of the situation washed over me, filling me with a profound sense of gratitude for the man who had stepped in to ensure my safety.

The road to recovery proved long and arduous, marked by countless medical procedures, scans, and surgeries. While my body bore the scars of that fateful night, the emotional wounds ran deeper.

One of the most challenging aspects of this ordeal was the realization that my mother would have to leave the hospital at night, leaving me alone in the solitude of my room. Nightfall brought with it a sense of vulnerability and isolation as I grappled with my fears and pain without her comforting presence.

As the hospital ward dimmed, the silence of the room echoed my thoughts, amplifying the weight of my predicament. It was in those moments, as darkness cloaked the world outside, that I felt truly alone.

Visions of the accident haunted my mind with fragmented memories refusing to merge into a coherent narrative. The emptiness within me mirrored the absence of answers.

Decades would pass before I could fully comprehend and come to terms with the emotional anguish and trauma I had endured. Now, years later, I can reflect on that fateful night with a profound sense of gratitude—gratitude for the neighbor whose swift actions rescued me from danger, for the dedicated medical professionals who tended to my recovery, and for the dear friend who made it her mission to check on me at home, who offered her support in the aftermath of the traumatic accident.

SEVEN

As the days neared Christmas, my excitement grew exponentially. It had always been my favorite holiday, and I cherished everything about it—the twinkling lights, the festive music, the cozy atmosphere. However, just a few days before Christmas, a dreadful incident occurred that could have easily tainted my love for the holiday season. Reflecting on it now, I am astounded by how I managed to maintain my joy for the holidays despite the impending turmoil.

My mother had wrapped several presents for my sisters and me, but with no space for a small Christmas tree or designated area for the gifts, she opted to place them at the end of my bed. Being a curious child, I couldn't resist the temptation to sneak a peek, inadvertently tearing the wrapping paper to glimpse inside. My mother quickly noticed the tampering and her demeanor shifted.

She turned around and looked at me, her eyes wide with anger. Her voice, which was usually gentle and soothing, turned into a deafening roar.

"¿Por qué chingados rompiste y abriste los regalos de Navidad?"

I froze and felt the blood drain from my face. I knew I had been caught. Terrified, I quickly answered by lying that it wasn't me who ripped the wrapping paper from the gifts. But my mother wasn't fooled.

"No mientas pendeja, ahora me dices qué fregados es."

I started crying, feeling cornered against the dresser in a fetal position, praying that she wouldn't hit me. This was not the first time I had experienced my mother's wrath, but this time was different. It was the moment that changed my view of the world forever.

I remember the fear that consumed me as I stood before my mother, desperately trying to convince her that I had no idea what was inside the gift. But she didn't believe me. Instead, she reached for the glue gun on top of the dresser and threatened me with it, demanding that I reveal the contents of the package.

I didn't know what to do. My mind raced as I tried to come up with a solution, but I couldn't think straight. I decided to stick to my original story and told her again that I didn't know what was inside the gift.

As soon as the words left my mouth, my mother's arm shot up, and I saw the long glue stick swing towards me. I covered my face with my arms and braced myself for impact. The pain was intense as the glue stick struck my legs, leaving long, red welts that burned with every strike.

I pleaded with my mother to stop, but she continued to hit me with the glue gun. In desperation, I told her it was a book, hoping that she would believe me and end the violence. But her rage only intensified, and I feared for my life.

As she continued to lash out at me, I wondered how I had ended up in this situation. How had my mother become so consumed with anger and violence that she would attack her own child? It was a question that would haunt me for years to come.

My mother's anger had always been unpredictable, and I never knew what would trigger it.

"No mientas estúpida, ¿qué me quieres ver la cara de pendeja?"

But this time, I had lied to her about the gift, and I knew I had pushed her too far. As she swung the glue gun towards me, I braced myself for the impact, my heart racing in my chest. When I finally opened my eyes, I saw the welts forming on my legs, and I knew it was going to be painful, but I also knew that I couldn't keep lying to her.

I blurted out the truth about the gift. "Son colores de agua para pintar."

To my surprise, she stopped hitting me and the room fell silent. I could feel the tears streaming down my face as I lay there on the ground unable to move.

When she turned and walked away, I slowly got up, wincing at the pain in my legs. I didn't know what to do next, so I just stood there, watching her disappear into the kitchen. It was only when I was sure she was gone that I finally let out a sob, the pain and fear of the past few minutes overwhelming me.

I made my way up the creaky ladder, the wood groaning under my weight as I ascended to the top of my bunk bed. I reached the summit and let out a sigh, my eyes drawn to the colorful Christmas presents waiting for me at the foot of my bed. I slumped onto the mattress, wiping away the tears that had been streaming down my face moments before.

As I sat there, a glint caught my eye, sparking my curiosity. Slowly, I crept towards the window, my fingers brushing against the curtain as I pulled it aside. My breath caught in my throat as I gazed out at the glittering night sky. The stars and sparkling lights twinkled like diamonds, beckoning me closer.

I leaned in, my nose pressed against the glass, my mind racing with wonder. Where did those stars lead? Where was this magical place? I whispered to myself, "¿Dónde están las luces? Ahí es donde quiero ir." The lights represented a destination I longed for, a place where my dreams could come alive.

As I sit here today, looking back on my childhood, I am filled with a deep sense of compassion and love for the little girl that I was. For so many years, I carried the weight of the trauma that I experienced, blaming myself for the pain that I endured. But now, I know that it was never my fault.

If you have undergone significant trauma during your childhood, please understand that you are not alone. These distressing experiences hold weight. You did not deserve to be mistreated or abused, and your pain is valid. It is possible to find healing and to move forward in a way that feels safe and empowering to you.

Choosing to love and care for yourself is one of the most powerful choices that you can make. It takes courage to face the pain and hurt of your past, but it is worth it. You deserve to feel safe, loved, and valued, and you have the power to create that for yourself.

I pray for the little girl inside of me, and for all of the children who have experienced trauma. I pray that we can all find healing and peace, and that we can learn to love and care for ourselves in the ways that we deserve. You are not alone, and you are worthy of love and compassion.

Illuminating Love and Faith:
A Prayer for Healing and Empowerment

I created this prayer for my own use, but I wanted to pass it on to you in case it can offer some solace during difficult moments.

Dear _____,

I pray for you to remember how much you are loved and to never lose faith in yourself or in life. May you always seek the light on your path, and, when you find it, may you open your heart and mind to nourish your spirit and guide you forward. May this light be shared with others, and may you continue to be a catalyst for healing for the next generation.

In times of fear, may you choose faith over fear and courage over doubt. May you always choose kindness and humbly accept the gifts you were born with, sharing them with the world in the name of love.

Nurturing Your Inner Child:
A Path to Healing and Self-Discovery

Dear Inner Child,

I want to take a moment to acknowledge you, to recognize the pain you may have endured, and to reassure you that you are loved and valued beyond measure. I know that there may have been times when you felt alone, scared, or unimportant, but I want you to know that those feelings don't define you. You are worthy of love, happiness, and all the good things life has to offer.

I understand that there may be wounds from the past that still hurt, but please know that you are not alone in this journey. I am here for you, to hold your hand through the tough times and celebrate with you during the joyful moments. Together, we can heal those wounds and learn to love and accept ourselves fully.

I want to remind you to be kind to yourself, just as you would be to a friend who is hurting. You deserve compassion, understanding, and patience. It's okay to feel your emotions and to take the time you need to process them. You are not weak for needing help or support; you are courageous for acknowledging your pain and taking steps towards healing.

Repeat after me: "I am loved and deserving of love. I am enough just as I am." These affirmations may feel unfamiliar at first, but with time and practice, they will become a source of strength and comfort for you. Believe in yourself, dear inner child, for you are worthy of all the love and happiness in the world.

If you ever feel overwhelmed or need someone to talk to, please don't hesitate to reach out for professional support. A therapist or counselor can provide you with the tools and guidance you need to navigate your feelings and experiences.

Remember, dear Inner Child, you are not defined by your past. You have the power to create a bright and beautiful future for yourself. Embrace your inner child, nurture them with love and care, and watch as they blossom into the amazing person you are meant to be.

With all my love,
Judy

Breaking Free from Negative Narratives: Reflective Questions for Healing Trauma

Take some time to reflect on your experiences of trauma and try to identify any negative narratives or beliefs that you have developed as a result. For example, you may believe that you are unlovable or that you are not worthy of happiness.

1. Think about how these narratives are holding your inner child hostage to the past. How are they preventing you from fully experiencing joy and connection in the present?

2. Consider whether these narratives are based in reality or if they are simply a result of your traumatic experiences. Try to challenge them with positive affirmations or counter-narratives that are more affirming and supportive.

3. Seek support from a therapist or counselor to work through any negative narratives or beliefs that are holding your inner child hostage to the past. They can help you to develop more positive and empowering narratives that allow you to move forward and experience more joy and fulfillment in your life.

Loving and Affirming Your Inner Child: Reflection Questions

1. Consider any negative self-talk that your inner child may be struggling with. How can you counter these negative beliefs with more positive and empowering messages?

2. Reflect on any past experiences that may have caused your inner child to doubt themselves or feel unworthy. What would you say to them now to help them move past these experiences and embrace their true selves?

3. Imagine that you have the opportunity to speak directly to your inner child. What would you say to them about who they are today? What positive affirmations would you offer them to counter any negative beliefs they may hold?

4. Think about how you can continue to nurture and support your inner child as you move forward in life. How can you ensure that they feel loved, valued, and heard?

Remember that healing from past trauma takes time and patience, and it's important to be gentle and compassionate with yourself as you navigate this process.

Self-Care Practice:
Give Yourself a Hug and Speak Kind Words

This is a positive and encouraging self-care practice that can help you feel comforted and supported. By giving yourself a hug, you are showing yourself love and care. Speaking kind words to yourself can help to counter any negative self-talk and improve your self-esteem. Even if it feels uncomfortable at first, practicing self-hugs and kind self-talk can gradually become more natural and comforting over time. Remember, you deserve love and kindness from yourself.

EIGHT

For most of my childhood, I had lived in a tiny room, feeling cramped and having no personal space of my own. However, things changed when I moved to the new apartment—a tall, white building situated on a corner between two streets: Grevillea Avenue and Lennox Boulevard. The two large palm trees just outside my bedroom window filled the air with the mouth-watering scent of freshly baked bread from the Gran Villa Bakery. I could also hear the music from our upstairs neighbor's apartment playing the melody "Querida, dime cuándo tú, dime cuándo tú, ah, ah."

It was moving day, and I couldn't help but feel a sense of disbelief. This was really happening. We were finally going to have our own place. No more cramped bedrooms, no more sharing a bathroom with neighbors. My heart was racing with excitement as I ran up and down the hallway of our new apartment. I couldn't wait to show my little sisters our new bedroom and all the space we now had.

As we stepped inside, the fresh paint and new carpet greeted us. It smelled clean and new, like the start of a new chapter in our lives. It was like a blank canvas waiting for us to fill it with new memories and laughter. I ran down the hallway, taking in every inch of our new home. I could feel the excitement bubbling up inside me, and I was filled with a sense of wonder and joy.

The sense of wonder and happiness that came with moving into our new apartment was short-lived, as it soon turned into a horrific nightmare on a warm summer night. It was shortly after my tenth birthday. My mother had just started working the graveyard shift at her new job to cover the higher rent and increased bills that came with the new place. Consequently, my stepdad had to take care of us during her absence. I recall my younger sisters being asleep in their beds when my stepdad asked me to join him in the bathtub, which was an unusual request. I followed him to the bathroom, as he was only wearing his underwear. He then suggested that I sit on his private parts, and the only thing I can remember from that moment is facing forward looking at the bath faucet and feeling the warm water running down my hands.

About the same time as the bathtub incident, I have a memory of another night when he asked if I wanted to play a game. Despite being young and naïve, I eagerly agreed. I dashed into the hallway to search for the board game "Snakes and Ladders," rummaging through the clutter in search of the missing dice. He came up to me quickly.

"No, not that game," he said.

Instead, he suggested we go to the bedroom, and he would show me a different game.

That very evening, I remember tossing and turning in my bed. I slept on the top bunk, and it would get very hot during the summer. One summer night, I abruptly woke up, looked to my right, and was startled to see him standing there. Looking directly at me, he smiled.

"I came to check in on you girls and make sure you are okay since you kick off your covers in the middle of night," he said.

I remember feeling paralyzed, not sure how to respond. My body felt tense as if I couldn't move. When my body finally was able to respond, I sat up and picked up my blanket at the end of my feet and mattress and quickly lifted it to my neck to cover my body.

Dressed in a sheer, lightweight gown, a necessity in our sweltering apartment, it would take over twenty-five years before I found the courage to reveal this buried memory to my therapist. The weight of guilt and shame from that fateful night had lingered, hidden deep within me, until I could no longer bear the burden alone.

As I reflect on my childhood, I come to understand that being a victim of sexual abuse was not my fault. It wasn't because of the clothes I was wearing or because I innocently said yes to playing a game with this person. It was because this person behaved in a way that violated my trust, safety, and well-being. I was just a child, with no real understanding of what was happening to me during that time.

This person had presented themselves as kind, warm, and caring. It was only years later that I learned about the grooming process and how it was used to gain the trust of their victims. It was heartbreaking to realize that someone I had trusted so much had betrayed me in such a terrible way.

For years, I had suppressed these memories, afraid to face them and say the words "I was sexually abused" aloud to myself. It was a painful process to go through the phases of grief, anger, sadness, confusion, and emotional turmoil. I had a lot of anger towards myself for many years because I continued to place this person on a pedestal for all the good deeds, how he supported our family for many years.

It was also difficult to face what had happened to me, and for many years, I stayed quiet because I was afraid to challenge the status quo. I did not want to create turmoil in our family because I was fearful of how it would impact and affect my relationships with my siblings.

As soon as I told my mother about the abuse I had experienced, I could see the shock and fear written all over her face. She kept asking me questions, and I could feel her desperation to understand what had happened. Even though it was overwhelming, I knew I had to tell her, not just for myself, but also to protect my younger siblings from the same fate.

It wasn't until many years later in a therapy session that I realized that my motivation to disclose the abuse to my mother was driven by my need to safeguard my siblings. Looking back, I know that I didn't have the language to fully articulate what I had gone through, but I'm grateful that I found the courage to speak up.

Judy Stella

NINE

As I sat in the living room, I could hear my mother's voice rising as she confronted my stepfather. Though I couldn't quite discern the exact conversation, I vividly recall the intensity of the moment. Despite my stepfather's attempts to dismiss it and calm my mother down, she was resolute. She demanded an explanation, and eventually, he conceded, accusing me of lying and asserting his innocence. He even went as far as suggesting he could be falsely accused and face legal repercussions.

I can't quite recollect my immediate feelings during that confrontation, but when I eventually mustered the courage to address it in therapy, the experience was painfully crushing to my soul. Even now, as I write this, a tidal wave of emotions overwhelms me. Anger, hurt, and frustration consume my thoughts as I grapple with the injustice of it all. I wish I had found my voice in that moment, but I was immobilized, concealed behind the couch, unable to move or speak.

My mother continued to confront my stepfather, demanding answers, and trying to make sense of what had happened. The arguing went on for what felt like hours, until my mother finally went to their bedroom and started throwing his belongings on the floor. She told him that he needed to leave the apartment, and he started frantically packing his things.

As he picked up his clothes and other belongings and put them in his van, I could see the worry and overwhelm written all over his face. He didn't sleep in the apartment that night, instead choosing to sleep in his car. The night my stepfather left our apartment and started sleeping in his van was a turning point for our family. His presence was gone, and things felt different, but the aftermath of the confrontation was something that I had not anticipated.

I remember the night vividly. It was after I had confided in my mother about the sexual abuse I had suffered. I was sound asleep when I was abruptly awoken by my mother's loud footsteps and screaming. In a state of confusion, I watched as she turned on my bedroom light, stripped my blanket off me, and grabbed me by the hair before pulling me off my bed. She yelled at me, using a string of slurs that I will never forget.

"Eres una sucia, estúpida, ni para limpiar tu cuarto sirves," she yelled. "No sirves para nada, así te has de limpiar el culo."

I was terrified and didn't understand what was happening. As I fell to the floor, I noticed my mother begin to pull out clothes from my closet and take out all my toys and anything else she could find, placing them in the center of my bedroom. She kept screaming, saying how dirty my room was, that I was going to clean it immediately.

My mother grabbed one of the hangers and charged towards me. I knew what was about to happen, and it was painful to admit that I had been in this situation before. I quickly curled up into a fetal position, shut my eyes tightly, and braced myself for the first hit. Seconds later, I felt the plastic hanger strike my leg, causing me to let out a loud cry. The blows continued to rain down on me, one after the other, until I was crying out in pain and begging her to stop.

I was terrified, thinking that she would never stop hitting me. But eventually, my mother grew tired and stopped, leaving me on the floor, whimpering with tears streaming down my cheeks.

"Limpia tu cochinero," she said looking at me before walking away and leaving me to clean up the mess.

I slowly tried to get up, but my legs were in so much pain from the beating that I cried even more. When I finally managed to stand up, I saw several vertical, swollen lines on my legs from the hanger. Looking back, I know that my mother was lashing out because of her own frustration and anger about the sexual abuse that I had disclosed to her. But at the time, I was just a scared and confused child, trying to make sense of what was happening to me.

Over thirty years have passed since that fateful summer, and as I reflect on my journey, I am proud of how far along I've come. One of the most important decisions I've made was finding the courage to confront what had happened to me.

For many years, I didn't connect the dots between the symptoms of my PTSD and the sexual abuse that I had endured. Life went on as if nothing had happened, but I was plagued by depression, anxiety, and a persistent feeling of emptiness. There were times when I would experience panic attacks triggered by certain conversations or by being in the presence of my abuser. Even becoming a mother brought on a new wave of emotional turbulence.

It wasn't until I sought therapy that I began to understand the true extent of the trauma I had experienced. The journey was not easy, but it was necessary for me to heal and move forward. Through therapy, I was able to confront the past and gain a deeper understanding of how the abuse had impacted my life.

I want others who have experienced sexual abuse to know that they are not alone. It can take time to recognize the symptoms of trauma and to understand the source of our pain, but with the right support and guidance, healing is possible. By facing our past, we can gain a greater sense of self-awareness and move forward with a renewed strength and hope for the future.

Looking back on my experiences, I realized that it's important to speak up and seek help when we are victims of abuse. It's not our fault, and we should never be ashamed to share our stories and seek solace. By speaking up, we not only help ourselves but also help others who may be going through similar experiences.

If you or someone you know has experienced sexual abuse, know that it's not your fault. Many times, our minds block out certain memories as a coping mechanism to protect us from further psychological harm.

As someone who has gone through several years of therapy, I have been able to face the few memories that I do remember with the support of a mental health professional. By uncovering and peeling back the layers of my pain and hurt, I gained a new understanding of how the incidents of sexual abuse impacted me throughout the years.

It was difficult to face and accept the harsh truth that for many years I had blamed myself for what had happened to me. I learned that this was a common response among many victims of sexual abuse. The truth is the perpetrator is the only one who needs to be held responsible for their actions and behaviors—never the victim.

Through therapy, I learned that it's important to be patient with ourselves as we heal. Healing from sexual abuse is a difficult and often lengthy process, but it is possible. We need to give ourselves permission to feel the pain, hurt, and anger that we may have buried deep within ourselves for years.

A Prayer of Solidarity and Support

Dear _____,

Today, I offer my prayers and stand with you in solidarity. Please know that you have my unwavering love and support. I understand that what has happened to you cannot be undone, but I pray that you will receive the comfort and courage to face the unfathomable pain.

May you experience true healing and find the boldness to walk the path towards inner peace. I pray that you recognize your worth and feel loved every day. May any false shame that you may feel or experience at times be eradicated from your life. Instead, may you find joy, hope, and peace.

May you fully comprehend and believe that the abuse is not your fault, and that your truth can set you free on your journey towards healing. May you be strengthened and empowered with courage and bravery to seek the help and support you need and deserve.

May everything come to light that will aid in your healing, and may you be led to receive the proper help. May you be encouraged and inspired by others who have been restored and transformed after experiencing abuse. Let us continue to gain strength and advocate for ourselves and those who have been hurt and wronged.

With love and support,
Judy

A Compassionate Approach: Reflection Questions for Survivors of Sexual Abuse on Their Healing Journey

1. How do you currently cope with the effects of the abuse on your life? Are these coping mechanisms helpful or harmful to your overall well-being?

2. What are some of the messages that you internalized about yourself as a result of the abuse? How have these messages impacted your sense of self-worth and your relationships with others?

3. Who are your support systems? How can you continue to build and strengthen these relationships to support your healing journey?

4. How do you currently feel about seeking professional help for your healing journey? What barriers might be preventing you from seeking this type of support and how can you overcome them?

5. What are some self-care practices that you can engage in to support your emotional and physical well-being on a regular basis? How can you prioritize these practices in your life moving forward?

TEN

A week after, things at home were quiet again as if nothing had happened. My mother started cooking dinner for him, washing his clothes, and ironing his uniform for work. As time went on, things returned to a sense of normalcy, and my stepfather's visits became more frequent. He was back to being a part of our daily lives, and I found myself feeling confused about how to feel. On one hand, I was relieved that the abuse had stopped, but on the other hand, I couldn't shake off the feeling that something was not right.

We never talked about what had happened that night or the abuse that I had experienced. The elephant in the room was too big to address, and it became a silent agreement that we all seemed to adhere to. But even though we never spoke about it, the abuse had left a lasting mark on our family dynamics, and things would never be the same again.

After the confrontation with my stepfather, a heavy burden settled upon my shoulders. It felt as though the weight of the world was pressing down on me, and I was left to deal with my emotions all on my own. There was no support system to lean on, no comforting voice to reassure me that everything would be okay.

I longed for someone to talk to, someone who would listen without judgment and offer solace in my time of need. But alas, there was no one. My mother, who should have been my pillar of strength, seemed oblivious to the turmoil brewing within me. She never asked how I was feeling, never inquired about the fear that had taken root in my heart.

Did she not hear the tremor in my voice, or see the flicker of anxiety in my eyes? Did she not understand the immense weight of having him back in our home? I wondered if she felt safe herself, or if her blind trust clouded her judgment. Perhaps she was too afraid to address the elephant in the room, afraid of the answers she might find.

There were countless unspoken questions that haunted my thoughts. Did my stepfather pose a threat to my safety? Would he ever repeat his abusive actions? I shuddered at the thought of enduring that pain again, the memories still fresh in my mind. But the silence prevailed. I swallowed my voice and left my fears unanswered.

The inner dialogue during that time was a tumultuous swirl of conflicting emotions and unanswered questions. Sitting around the dining table with my family, the mere presence of my stepfather ignited a flurry of thoughts. How should I act? How should I behave when he comes over for dinner? The uncertainty of it all weighed heavily upon me.

Avoiding eye contact became my survival strategy, a way to shield myself from his gaze and the discomfort it stirred within me. I couldn't bear to look into his eyes, fearing that they held secrets and intentions that I dared not uncover. The table became a battleground of unspoken tension, each moment charged with unexpressed thoughts and unacknowledged pain.

Do I still call him Dad? The question echoed in my mind, lingering in the silence between us. The word felt foreign on my lips, a hollow designation that carried little meaning. The bond of father and child had been shattered by his actions, and I grappled with the confusion of whether I should continue using a term that held such heavy connotations.

And how was I supposed to feel when he treated me kindly and smiled at me? Conflicting emotions tugged at my heartstrings. On one hand, his moments of warmth and affection sparked a flicker of hope within me. Perhaps, I thought, he had changed. Perhaps there was goodness buried beneath the layers of darkness. But beneath that glimmer of hope, a deep-rooted distrust and fear lingered. I couldn't fully embrace his kindness, always wary of the hidden motives that may lie beneath.

When he got too close to me, my discomfort would intensify. I wished he would maintain his distance, physically and emotionally. The boundaries between us had been shattered, and his proximity sent ripples of unease through my entire being. I longed for space, for safety, for the ability to breathe freely without the weight of his presence suffocating me.

"Stop talking," I would silently plead. "Stop sounding like you are a caring person, while the scars of your actions still haunt me." The words he spoke carried an air of false sincerity, and I yearned for honesty and authenticity. The dissonance between his words and his past deeds tore at my fragile sense of trust.

In the depths of my being, I harbored a fervent wish. I wished he would just go away and never return to our home. I yearned for a life free from his influence, a life where my family could heal and rebuild without the constant reminder of his presence.

Amidst the chaos of unanswered questions and conflicting emotions, I held onto a sliver of strength. It was a strength that whispered to me, encouraging me to find my voice, to reclaim my power, and to forge my own path towards healing. Though the silence persisted, I knew deep within that one day, I would find the courage to break it, to confront the questions that haunted my thoughts, and to find the answers I so desperately sought.

ELEVEN

I yearned for an outlet, a release from my anger, from the hurt, and sadness that consumed me. But in the confines of my solitary struggle, I realized there was no one coming to my rescue. I believe this is where my passion for reading books began.

Today, as I reflect on my journey and the impact of reading on my life, I find myself sharing a half-joking, half-serious confession: my first self-help book was *"Alexander and the Terrible, Horrible, No Good, Very Bad Day."* In a way, it's a lighthearted nod to the power of literature to provide solace and guidance, even in unexpected places.

As a child, I resonated with Alexander's story of a day gone awry. It was a tale of frustration, disappointment, and a longing for better days. In my own life, I faced challenges and hardships that seemed insurmountable. But within the pages of that simple children's book, I found a glimmer of hope.

Every weekend morning, I would wake up and make my way to the kitchen, feeling a familiar sense of anticipation bubbling within me. As I poured myself a bowl of cereal, my mind already buzzing with excitement, I knew that my true destination was not outside, among friends or in the bustling world. No, my true sanctuary awaited me in my own bedroom.

With my bowl of cereal finished, I would hurry back to my bed, eager to immerse myself in the world within the pages of a book. As I nestled under the covers, I would open the book that lay beside me, its worn pages and familiar scent providing a sense of comfort. The outside world would fade away as I delved into the story before me.

Hours would slip by unnoticed, as I lost myself in the captivating tales that unfolded on the pages. Adventures, mysteries, and fantastical worlds became my companions, transporting me far away from the hardships of my own life. The characters within the books felt like friends, their triumphs and struggles intertwined with my own.

In the quiet solitude of my room, I could escape the chaos and find solace. The weight of the abuse, the strained family dynamics, and the unspoken words would temporarily dissipate as I embarked on literary journeys. With each turn of the page, I discovered new realms of courage, resilience, and hope.

Reading was not just a hobby, it was my lifeline. It nurtured my imagination, expanded my horizons, it offered a glimpse into what a better life could be–a gateway to infinite possibilities. It provided an escape from the pain and a temporary respite from reality. Within the world of books, I found strength, inspiration, and the belief that there was more to life than what I had experienced.

As I lost myself in the stories, I felt a renewed sense of purpose. Reading fueled my passion for knowledge, deepened my understanding of the human experience, and reminded me of the power of storytelling. It became a source of strength, a constant reminder that I was not alone, and that there was hope beyond the struggles I faced.

Even now, as an adult, my love for reading is very much present with me today. It's become a lifelong companion, a sanctuary I could always return to and feel inspired by. It guided me through the darkest of times and continues to accompany me on my journey of healing and growth. It taught me the resilience of the human spirit, the importance of finding my voice, and the endless possibilities that exist within the pages of a book.

TWELVE

Despite the overwhelming weight of my circumstances, there was a flicker of strength within me that refused to be extinguished. That strength stemmed from my deep love and sense of responsibility for my younger sisters. In their innocent faces, I found purpose and a reason to keep pushing forward.

They became my anchor, my reason to keep showing up every day. The weight of responsibility settled upon my young shoulders, and although no child should have to bear such immense responsibility, I felt a deep gratitude for the role I had in their lives. It was an immense task, one that required me to grow up faster than my years should have allowed.

Taking care of my sisters gave me a sense of purpose, a reason to push through the darkness that surrounded us. It was a reminder that I had something to protect, something to fight for. In the face of uncertainty and fear, their innocent smiles and laughter became my guiding light.

The term "parentified child" would come to resonate with me later on, as I learned about the psychological impact of having more responsibility than the average child. People would tell me that I was mature for my age, that I carried the weight of a caregiver. While it was a heavy burden to bear, it also saved me from possibly going down a darker path.

Amidst the chaos and pain, caring for my sisters gave me a sense of stability and purpose. It provided a semblance of normalcy in a situation that was anything but normal. I would cook meals for them, make sure they were safe, and offer them the love and support that I yearned for myself.

As I reflect on those challenging times, I recognize the strength that blossomed within me through my role as a caretaker. It wasn't an ideal circumstance, but it instilled in me a resilience and determination that would guide me on my journey of healing and growth.

Today, I am grateful for the opportunity to be a positive role model for my sisters and brother. They are my motivation to continue a journey of healing and personal growth. The responsibility I once carried on my young shoulders has transformed into a commitment to create a better future for both myself and them.

THIRTEEN

As life continued to unfold, once again, I found solace in the kindness of a teacher-turned-mentor. Ms. Sopa, my fifth grade teacher, became more than just a mentor to me; she was a guiding light, forever engraving herself upon my heart. Stepping into her classroom for music class was like entering an igloo, the chill enveloping me. But I didn't mind the cold; her presence made it worthwhile. Her warm smile and genuine care created a safe haven in her classroom.

During our music lessons, Ms. Sopa shared her love for various genres, but it was her admiration for Elvis Presley that resonated with me the most. Looking back, I realize that her passion for rock and roll music must have influenced my own burgeoning interest in the genre. She unknowingly sparked a flame within me, igniting a love for music that would also carry me through difficult times.

As the end of fifth grade approached, I was saddened by the thought of leaving Ms. Sopa behind as I transitioned into middle school. I couldn't imagine starting my next chapter in life without her, without being able to see her warm and endearing smile. During the darkest period of my life, her warm smile and genuine care had provided me with reassurance and stability.

However, fate had a different plan in store for me. During my first week of middle school, I discovered that Ms. Sopa would be teaching there as well. It felt as though my prayers had been answered. Her presence became a source of comfort as I navigated the challenges of this new chapter. Every lunch break, I would seek refuge in her classroom, offering my help and feeling embraced by her warm greeting. On my birthday, she surprised me with a custom-made card, reminding me that my presence mattered to someone. In her classroom, I felt seen, loved, and like I had a place in the world.

During middle school, I joined a youth program where important life skills were imparted, such as resume building and personal development. At the program's completion ceremony, I invited Ms. Sopa. I will never forget the sight of her walking in and taking a seat among the audience, her smile radiating pride and support. After the ceremony, she congratulated me with a warm hug and handed me a gift bag. Inside, I discovered a beautiful yellow flower glass paperweight, an angel-shaped pen, and a 5x7 scripture passage with my name in the center. The scripture Psalm 145:3 became a cherished treasure. Over the years, in moments of struggle, I would hold it close, finding comfort in its words.

A few years ago, driven by a deep gratitude and a desire to express my appreciation, I began searching for Ms. Sopa, hoping for a reunion. Unfortunately, I received the heartbreaking news from an old classmate that she had passed away. The weight of the loss hit me like a wave, and I sought comfort in my therapy sessions to process the grief.

Though she is no longer physically present, Ms. Sopa's impact on my life remains profound. Her kindness, guidance, and unwavering support served as a beacon of light during my darkest days. The memories we shared, the lessons she taught, and the warmth of her smile continue to shape my journey.

In my heart, I carry the gratitude I wish I could have expressed to her personally, and as I reflect on her legacy, I am reminded of the importance of kindness, mentorship, and the profound impact that a caring soul can have on another's life. Ms. Sopa's memory lives on, forever imprinted on my heart, a reminder of the power of compassion and the enduring influence of a teacher who truly cares.

FOURTEEN

From my earliest memories, the importance of hard work was instilled in me. Each day, I would rise and immediately begin the tasks and chores that awaited me, taking on the responsibilities of caring for my younger siblings. Even on the days when we went to the park for a brief respite, my mother would have me rummage through the trash bins for soda cans and bottles. By the time we left the park, our small trash bag would be filled to the brim.

On weekends, she would lead me to the side of the house, instructing me to crush the cans with my feet and separate the aluminum cans from the glass bottles. I would spend three to four hours on a Saturday morning meticulously carrying out this task. Once finished, we would head to a nearby recycling center to exchange the cans for cash. Sometimes, as a treat, my mother would take my siblings and me to our favorite spot: Jim's Burgers. The anticipation of that meal filled me with excitement, and I eagerly prepared the table with napkins and small plates while she cut the burgers in half for us to share.

Collecting recyclables was not the only means through which we navigated our financial struggles. There was a time when my mother found temporary work at a laundromat. Her job involved ensuring that all customers were out before closing time. Some of these tasks were assigned to me, such as brushing the soap off and meticulously drying and wiping down the machine lids while she swept the floors free of debris. Then I would have to wait while she mopped the entire space.

On several nights I offered to take on more responsibilities to finish more quickly. My mother would hand me a broom, and we would sweep together—one side for her, and the other for me. Often, we would patiently wait for the last customer to finish so she could lock the doors and begin mopping the floors. By then, it would be past 10 PM, and she would instruct me to lie down on a bench, waiting for her to finish. Fatigue and exhaustion would consume me, and I would curl up on the bench, shivering in the cold. After approximately forty minutes, my mother would gently nudge my shoulder, waking me up with her words.

"Vámonos ya, es hora de irnos a la casa." At that time, my mother didn't have a car, so we would walk late at night for six blocks–from El Lennox Pollo on Inglewood Avenue to La Gran Villa Bakery on Grevillea Avenue.

One particular night, as we turned the corner on Lennox Boulevard, we stumbled upon an empty shopping cart. With a tired smile and a nod of her head, my mother gestured toward the cart.

"Ándale, súbete al carrito y yo te paseo hasta la casa," she said. I happily climbed into the cart, grateful for the respite from the physical strain and for the small moment of joy it brought during those challenging times.

Upon arriving home, I would hastily kick off my shoes, foregoing changing into pajamas or brushing my teeth. Exhausted from a long day at school followed by late-night work at the laundromat, I would collapse into bed. The next morning, my mother's voice would rouse me from my slumber with her familiar wake-up call.

"Judy, ya levántate, es hora para ir a la escuela."

The cycle of hard work and perseverance continued, woven into the fabric of our daily lives. Despite the challenges we faced, I held onto a glimmer of hope, knowing that each day brought new possibilities and a chance to shape a brighter future. And within those moments of struggle, I found strength and resilience, guided by my mother's strong work ethic and determination.

FIFTEEN

We moved to a new house on Dalerose Avenue, and I fell in love with it immediately. Our new home brought with it a sense of serenity for me, a peaceful escape from the turbulent environment that consumed our home. My mother's mood swings and emotional abuse were a constant storm, but amidst it all, the front lawn with its beautiful green grass, lemon tree, and colorful flowers offered a safe haven. Each evening, I found solace in the act of watering the flowers and breathing in the fresh air, a respite from the challenges that plagued our home due to my mother's unstable mood changes and emotional abuse.

As fate would have it, another family moved into the back house a few months after we settled in. They were a peculiar bunch—an older woman and her three sons. One of them, the youngest, caught my attention one fateful day when he strolled through the driveway while I was throwing the trash away. Our eyes met, and I felt a rush of nerves that left me speechless. He greeted me with a warm smile and a wave, but I quickly retreated into my house, unsure of how to respond.

Yet, fate had other plans, and we kept bumping into each other. With each encounter, my nervousness began to wane, and we eventually struck up conversations. He was friendly and had an easygoing charm that put me at ease. We discovered a shared love for sports, cheering for the same baseball and basketball teams—the Dodgers and the Lakers, respectively.

As our interactions continued, I couldn't help but develop feelings for him. He made me feel seen and heard, something I had been yearning for amid the emotional turmoil at home. I craved attention and affection, and he seemed willing to provide it. However, there was a significant obstacle in the way of our potential relationship—he was six years older than me and belonged to a local gang.

I knew my mother would never approve of our friendship, let alone a romantic relationship. His background and lifestyle clashed with her expectations for me. But adolescent love knows no boundaries, and despite the risks, I agreed to be his girlfriend in secret.

We had to be careful, sneaking phone calls when my mother wasn't around, creating elaborate ruses to hide our meetings, and even missing school just to spend time together. I would pretend to be sick, fabricating notes to excuse my absences, all for the sake of being with him. At night, we'd meet clandestinely on my windowsill after my mother had fallen asleep, just to steal a few moments together.

Our secret meetings became our lifeline, a sanctuary where we could express our feelings freely. He showered me with compliments, telling me how much he liked me and how lucky he was to have such a pretty girlfriend. For a time, the excitement of young love kept us afloat, oblivious to the storm brewing around us.

But as with all secrets, ours couldn't remain hidden forever. One night, my mother unexpectedly woke up and heard voices coming from my room. She decided to investigate, creeping around the side of the house and catching us off guard. In a panic, he vanished into the night, leaving me exposed and vulnerable.

My mother's fury was unleashed upon me as she dragged me into the living room, hurling a barrage of hurtful words. She slapped me across the face, leaving me stunned and in tears. She forbade me from ever seeing him again, deeming him a low-life gang member unworthy of my company.

Our clandestine meetings came to an abrupt halt, and my bedroom window was sealed shut with a dresser and a tall mirror, ensuring that we could no longer communicate in secret. I was trapped, torn between my love for him and my loyalty to my mother.

As time went on, I discovered that he had lied about his age, revealing himself to be eight years older than me. The depth of his deception hit me like a tidal wave, leaving me wondering if our love story was nothing more than a dream built on a foundation of lies.

Yet, the pull of forbidden love was too strong to ignore. Despite the obstacles and the pain, I found myself unable to let go. The heart wants what it wants, and my heart was entangled with his in a love that defied reason and societal norms. Little did I know that our tumultuous journey was only just the beginning.

Judy Stella

SIXTEEN

Several months passed, and it seemed that my mother had come to realize that her strict approach to forbidding our relationship was only pushing me further away. She must have seen that her threats of sending me away did not phase me, and she feared I might run off with him if she didn't find a middle ground.

For the next three years, she loosened her grip on our relationship, allowing us limited time together on the front porch if my homework and chores were completed. Sometimes, she even granted us permission to go out for lunch, and we would walk to a nearby fast-food restaurant to share a meal.

During those years, however, my boyfriend began to exhibit troubling behaviors. His drinking habits grew excessively, leading to verbal and emotional abuse. He started to control how I dressed, forbidding makeup, and limiting interactions with other males at school. His jealousy reached dangerous levels, becoming furious at the mere thought of me being interested in someone else.

One night, his jealousy boiled over, and things took a dark turn. My mother unexpectedly entered my room and found him with his hand around my throat, threatening me if I dared to leave the house without his permission. It was a terrifying and eye-opening moment, but my feelings for him were still tangled in a complex web of emotions.

As time passed, I turned sixteen, but my life was about to change drastically. I began feeling sick, experiencing nausea and a sudden loss of appetite. My mother took me to the local community clinic, where the doctor asked if there was any chance I could be pregnant. I panicked and gave a false date of my last period, hoping to dismiss any suspicions.

However, the truth couldn't stay hidden for long. His sisters took me to another community clinic where I received the confirmation that I was indeed pregnant. I was scared, unsure of what to do next, but when I shared the news with my boyfriend, we surprisingly found a moment of joy together, embracing the prospect of a new baby.

The fear of telling my mother loomed over us, and we postponed the inevitable conversation, terrified of her reaction. I knew she would be disappointed, and I feared she might kick me out of the house. With each passing week, it became harder to conceal the truth. I rushed to the mall and bought bigger-sized clothes to hide my growing bump, but I knew my petite frame wouldn't be able to conceal it for much longer.

Eventually, the day came when I could no longer keep the secret to myself. The nausea had ceased, but the reality of my pregnancy was evident. I steeled myself for the conversation, knowing that it would be one of the most difficult moments of my life.

SEVENTEEN

The weekend that followed was a harrowing chapter engraved deeply into the fabric of my memories—a stark portrayal of pain and fear that would shake my world. As I lay in bed, I began to feel an unsettling sensation in my lower abdomen and noticed the ominous signs of spotting. Panic seized me, and I knew I couldn't face this alone. Desperate for comfort and assurance, I reached out to my boyfriend, but he was nowhere to be found. Tears streamed down my face as I felt the cramps intensify, coming in short waves every twenty minutes. I was terrified, and the world around me seemed to collapse under the weight of uncertainty. With no one to turn to, I confided in a friend who offered to take me to the hospital. There, I underwent tests and an ultrasound, only to receive heartbreaking news: the fetus did not have a heartbeat, and my pregnancy hormone levels were dangerously low for the weeks I had reported.

The doctor informed me there was nothing they could do, and I would need a D & C procedure. Confused and overwhelmed, the pain in my lower abdomen grew more intense as I lay there, uncertain of what the future held. Hours passed, and I found myself waiting in agony for the procedure, feeling alone and afraid.

So many thoughts were going through my mind. What's happening to me? I couldn't comprehend the reality of what was unfolding within me. What happened to my baby? What did I do wrong? I racked my brain, searching for answers and blaming myself for something I couldn't understand. The guilt weighed heavily on my heart, and I wished I had gone to the doctor earlier, thinking that maybe I could have prevented this tragedy.

As the hours dragged on, the pain intensified, and the contractions became unbearable, causing me to scream with each new wave. During one particularly agonizing contraction, I suddenly felt a tremendous burst, and a rush of water gushed down my legs, leaving me terrified and bewildered by the sudden and unfamiliar sensations coursing through my body.

Suddenly, my boyfriend walked in, disheveled and reeking of alcohol. I summoned the courage to share the medical prognosis with him, hoping for support and understanding, but he remained silent and distant. His lack of care cut deep, and as he turned to leave, I called after him in desperation, but he left me at the hospital, abandoned and heartbroken.

In the midst of my anguish, I overheard nurses expressing concern, wondering where my mother was and if they should report my situation to Child Protective Services. Fearing the consequences, I reluctantly provided my mother's contact information.

Finally, my mother arrived, and I couldn't hold back the flood of tears. Guilt and shame washed over me as I apologized for my situation. With her comforting presence, I was moved to a different floor and prepared for the D & C procedure. My mother assured me she would be waiting for me, providing a glimmer of comfort in my darkest hour.

As I entered the cold operating room, fear gripped me, and I was given anesthesia. The next thing I knew, I was waking up feeling weak and vulnerable. My mother and my boyfriend stood by my side, but the silence in the room was heavy with unspoken emotions.

Returning home that night, no one spoke a word in the car. The weight of my experience weighed heavily on all of us. As we entered the living room, my mother made it clear that we would keep this incident hidden from my stepfather.

"No le vamos a decir a tu papá ni una palabra de esto," she said. A shroud of secrecy enveloped us, and I retreated to my room, aching physically and emotionally.

The days that followed were filled with a sense of loss and sorrow that permeated everything. The pain in my body would heal, but the wounds in my heart would take longer to mend. I yearned for consolation and healing, yet the shadows of solitude engulfed me, leaving me to navigate the aftermath of this traumatic experience on my own.

EIGHTEEN

A week had passed since that fateful night at the hospital. Life had resumed its regular rhythm, but the weight of the experience still lingered, haunting my thoughts during my shifts at McDonald's and in moments of solitude. One night, after finishing my late shift, my mother offered to pick me up. As we drove slowly on Lennox Boulevard, the familiar streets seemed to hold the memories of my pain and fear.

Then, my mother broke the silence with a question that pierced my heart, bringing me back to the painful night and fears from the hospital.

"¿Por qué no me dijiste que estabas embarazada?" (Why didn't you tell me you were pregnant?)

Her voice was gentle, but I felt the shame and guilt wash over me once more. I wanted to face her, to look into her eyes and find solace, but I couldn't bring myself to do it. Instead, I kept my gaze fixed on the passing streetlights as I mustered a response.

My voice trembled, and tears welled up in my eyes, threatening to spill over as I replied.

"Porque tenía miedo de tu reacción, miedo de que me echaras de la casa." (Because I was afraid of your reaction, afraid you'd kick me out of the house.)

Admitting my fear out loud made my emotions overflow, and tears streamed down my cheeks.

For a moment, I braced myself, anticipating anger or disappointment, but to my astonishment, my mother's hand reached out not to harm me but to offer comfort. As we drove by our old apartment, a rush of memories flooded in, but there was no harsh criticism or scolding. I had closed my eyes, expecting the worst, but instead, she offered me comfort and love. She pulled me closer, wrapping her arm around me, and we both began to cry. She reassured me. "¿Cómo puedes pensar que te echaría? Eres mi hija y te amo."(How could you think I'd ever kick you out? You are my daughter, and I love you.)

Her words pierced through the darkness that had clouded my heart, and the dam of emotions burst forth. We both cried together, releasing the pain and fear that had been bottled up. The warmth of her embrace and the sincerity in her words lifted a weight I hadn't known I carried. In that moment, the night sky above us seemed to hold a new light, and the moon's gentle glow offered a glimmer of hope.

Once again, I realized that it was at this same location where I had experienced the most painful moments. It was the place where my mother's actions had inflicted so much pain, where my sense of safety had been shattered, and where the name "liar" had cut deep. Yet, here, under the moonlight, a transformation had taken place, and this place was becoming a symbol of healing.

Reflection Questions

1. What specific memories or interactions with your mother trigger feelings of pain or discomfort?

2. How has your relationship with your mother influenced your self-perception and sense of worth?

3. Are there any patterns or behaviors in your current relationships that seem to echo the dynamics of your relationship with your mother?

4. What aspects of yourself have you hidden or suppressed due to the pain from your relationship with your mother?

Remember that healing from mother wounds takes time and self-compassion. These reflection questions can serve as a starting point for your journey of self-discovery and healing, but seeking professional guidance, such as therapy, can provide invaluable support in navigating this complex process.

Affirmations

1. "I am deserving of love, compassion, and healing, independent of my past experiences with my mother."

2. "I release the burdens of the past and embrace the freedom to create a joyful and fulfilling life for myself."

3. "I am actively nurturing a loving and nurturing relationship with myself, allowing healing and growth to flourish within me."

Remember, affirmations are most effective when practiced regularly and with genuine belief. As you repeat these affirmations, visualize the positive changes you're inviting into your life and cultivate a sense of acceptance and healing.

Judy Stella

NINETEEN

As we continued our journey home, I found myself gazing at the moon above, its gentle glow casting a hopeful light upon my troubled soul. It was on this night that something profound shifted within me, though I couldn't fully grasp the depth of its impact at the time.

It would take another twenty years for the true significance of that night to unfold. It was in a regularly scheduled therapy session that I found the strength to revisit the painful memories of my miscarriage. The emotions that had lain dormant for so long came roaring back, like a torrential waterfall of grief.

In the safety of my therapist's office, I felt my voice trembling, my tears flowing freely, and my heart aching with the weight of loss and guilt. For years, I had blamed myself, believing that somehow, I was responsible for not having my baby with me. With hands covering my tear-stained face, my entire being ached with agony, a cry of pain erupted from the depths of my soul.

"I planned on having a baby, and I went home that night without my baby."

The words poured out, raw and unfiltered, like a catharsis of emotions that had been pent up for years. And with every tear shed, I felt a piece of my burden slowly lifted, replaced by a sense of relief and forgiveness—forgiveness towards myself for a loss that was never my fault.

And in that very same session, the pieces of my life's puzzle began to fall into place. It was the love and acceptance I had felt from my mother that night on Lennox Boulevard that had unlocked a hidden chamber within my heart. I realized that I couldn't recall her ever saying "I love you" before.

By the end of that session, I felt changed, lighter somehow. The burden of secrecy and shame that I had carried for so long had been lifted. It is in this moment of revelation that I realize the profound impact that night with my mother had on me. Hearing her say she loved me, perhaps for the first time, instilled in me a newfound sense of love and self-worth.

In the wake of that profound night with my mother, an unexpected transformation was set into motion. Empowered by the love she had shown me, I began to dig deep into my own well of self-worth and self-love. It was as if the seeds of strength that she had planted had finally taken root within me, a comforting warmth enveloped me, wrapping me in a cocoon of safety and love. For the first time, I felt truly acknowledged and valued, realizing that my presence held significance in my mother's heart.

The courage I found within myself became the catalyst for the most significant decision of all: to finally sever the toxic ties that had bound me to my abusive boyfriend. This was no impulsive action; it was a conscious declaration of self-respect and self-preservation. I was determined that this would be the end of the cyclical pattern, no more falling into the trap of breaking up and making up.

Summoning my newfound strength, I dialed his number, my heart resolute, and my voice steady as I declared that I could no longer continue in a relationship that brought me only pain. With unwavering clarity, I told him it was over, that I no longer wished to be in his grip, and I implored him to respect my decision and leave me alone. The weight of the words carried a sense of finality, and in that moment, I knew I was choosing myself over everything else.

With that phone call, I broke the chains that had bound me for so long. And as the line went quiet, I felt a rush of emotions — relief, liberation, but also a glimmer of hope. I had taken the first steps towards my healing journey, and there was no turning back. From that point on, I focused all my energy on moving forward, on building a life that was free from the shadows of the past.

And so, with the moon as my constant companion, I navigated the uncharted waters of my healing journey. Each night sky held a promise of a brighter tomorrow, a tomorrow where the scars of the past were being gradually replaced by vibrant hues of hope. The road ahead was uncertain, but armed with self-love, newfound strength, and the echoes of my mother's love.

Judy Stella

TWENTY

The summer came to an end, painting the skies with hues of warm orange and dusky purples. It was a bittersweet farewell to the days of leisure and a welcoming hello to new beginnings. I prepared to return to school. It was my senior year at Hawthorne High School in the city of Hawthorne, California. My heart was brimming with a mix of emotions from excitement and a touch of nerves for the unknown. This was the beginning of a new chapter, one that I was determined to embrace with all my might.

Back in the bustling walkways of school, the familiar faces of friends greeted me. The joy of reuniting with them after the summer break was infectious. I felt a renewed sense of belonging, a realization that I was not alone on this journey. As I settled into the rhythm of classes, I knew that this year was pivotal, a bridge to the next chapter of my life.

With unwavering determination, I charted a path towards college. My schedule was packed with challenging college prep courses, each one a stepping stone towards my dreams. But what excited me most were those lunch breaks spent in the college center, a place filled with information and opportunities. It was here that I would meet Harrelson, the college guidance counselor, who would become an unexpected guiding light on my journey.

Harrelson's presence was commanding, his tall frame and serious demeanor contrasting with the gentle tone he used to answer my questions. Patient and willing to help, he would soon become more than just a counselor; he was my mentor, and the person to whom I gave full credit for my success. I learned that he had walked a similar path, once a graduate of the same high school, now back to offer support and guidance as part of his community outreach role as an EOP counselor at Cal State University Long Beach.

Under his mentorship, the path to college seemed clearer. He took me under his wing, offering insights, guidance, and unwavering support. Looking back, I realize that he played a crucial role in shaping my future. As a first-generation high school graduate, the road to higher education was uncharted territory for me. Excitement and nerves mingled as I placed my trust in Harrelson's kindness and expertise. I lacked older siblings, family members, or friends who could serve as role models, but Harrelson stepped into that role with grace.

Beyond the classroom, Harrelson continued to be my anchor. The college application process, with its complexities and uncertainties, became less daunting with his guidance. His wisdom and encouragement fueled my determination, propelling me forward despite the challenges that lay ahead.

As the days passed, senior year transformed into graduation day, a culmination of years of hard work and dedication. With my cap and gown, I stood tall among my peers, a symbol of triumph against adversity. As I received my diploma, I knew that this was just the beginning. The summer after graduation, leading into my first semester of college, was a period of both eagerness and trepidation.

The transition from high school to college was both exhilarating and nerve-racking, but I was armed with knowledge, resilience, and the memory of his guidance. I remained in touch with Harrelson, updating him on my college journey, seeking advice, and sharing my successes and challenges. His role in my life extended beyond a high school counselor; he became a lifelong mentor, a pivotal force that illuminated my path and instilled in me the belief that I had it in me to pursue a higher education.

As the years passed on, his influence continued to shape my choices and aspirations. Harrelson had not just helped me navigate the journey to college, he had given me the tools to navigate life itself. With gratitude in my heart, I moved forward, knowing that his guidance had forever changed the trajectory of my story.

TWENTY ONE

As the warm embrace of another summer drew near, my days transformed into a delightful routine. The sun-kissed beach became my sanctuary, the cozy corners of my cherished bookstore–my haven–and the evening shifts that filled my week and weekends struck a perfect harmony between leisure and responsibility.

I found myself eagerly looking forward to my workdays. During this phase, I occupied the role of a cashier at Marie Callender's, a place that held a special space in my heart. But what made my heart race with anticipation was the approaching milestone of my eighteenth birthday. Alongside the candles on my cake, a new chapter was about to open. I was set to begin my journey towards becoming a server. The prospect of this upgrade filled me with excitement. It promised a greater share of responsibilities–and, of course, the chance to amass a heftier income through tips–all while serving the smiling faces that would grace our tables.

Yet, it wasn't just about the financial possibilities that made my job exciting. The true gems were the people who colored the canvas of my working life. Among them, the memory of Alex shone brightly. Her initial smile and warm embrace, when she held the role of cashier, stamped a special place in my heart. She became a wellspring of support and encouragement, a memory I carry forward, hoping that one day she might stumble upon my story and realize the profound impact she had on my life's transition.

Over the years, I formed connections with countless souls at Marie's. Some breezed through for a short while, while others remained steadfast, just like the rhythm of the tides against the shore. The bond shared among the kitchen staff, servers, and the unwavering commitment of my cherished bussers, Enrique and Efrain, eased the burden of my busiest days waiting tables. Those familiar with the serving industry understand the frenetic pace and demands of managing a full station simultaneously. But with both by my side, that chaos became a symphony of teamwork. And in return for their steadfast assistance, I ensured their pockets were well-lined with their fair share of the night's tips.

Then, there was Agustin, lovingly known as Auggie—a figure whose kindness flowed as naturally as a river's current. Auggie wasn't just a co-worker or friend even, he had a heart of gold that exuded such nurturing positivity. He guided me through the intricacies of exceptional customer service, a skill I hold dear and attribute to his tutelage. But Auggie's story, like a well-guarded secret, will be unveiled in due time. For now, his introduction alone does justice to his remarkable presence.

Time passed in a beautiful blur as I formed and cultivated many beautiful friendships that I treasure to this very day. The friendships nurtured amidst the aroma of freshly baked pies and sizzling dishes encapsulated my formative years, complete with the growing pains that accompany them. These memories paved the path that led me to my next adventure—a journey as a college student at Cal State University Long Beach.

TWENTY TWO

The morning sun cast a warm glow as I set out on a journey that held the promise of new beginnings. With a mixture of excitement and anxiety, I merged onto the 405 South Freeway, my heart racing along with the cars around me. The campus of Cal State Long Beach awaited my presence, and I was determined to make it to my freshman orientation on time.

As the wheels of my car hummed along the blacktop, I marveled at the feeling of freedom that driving on a freeway provided. Though I had never ventured onto these fast-moving lanes before, my determination to succeed fueled my courage. Leaving my house early, I allowed myself an extra cushion of time, aware that I was embarking on a new journey into the unknown.

However, my journey took an unexpected turn when I found myself on the wrong freeway. The 710-freeway beckoned me, its signs reading "Long Beach." However, my gut feeling whispered that something was amiss. Recognizing my mistake, I swiftly took the first exit and parked by the side of the road. In that moment, the isolation hit me. Alone and off course, I confronted a daunting truth: I was truly scared.

Drawing strength from within, I dialed Harrelson's number, and asked for help. His voice was a lifeline, offering specific instructions to navigate my way back on to the right road. Following his guidance, I made a left on Bellflower Boulevard. Minutes later, the towering blue pyramid of Cal State Long Beach emerged, igniting a spark of excitement within me again.

Guided by the sight of that landmark, I turned into the parking lot. I gathered my backpack and campus map, determined not to let uncertainty lead me astray again. With a heart racing from both exhilaration and nerves, I stepped onto the campus, ready to embrace this new chapter.

Walking into the classroom, I clung to my backpack like a security blanket. My outfit, a pair of dark blue jeans and a white shirt, was the armor I wore to face the unfamiliar. As my eyes darted around, I spotted an empty seat by the door, a safe haven of sorts. Taking a seat, my heart continued its wild dance as I anxiously awaited the start of my first college class.

The professor entered, an older figure with an air of intelligence about him. He welcomed us warmly, distributing a syllabus to each desk. When he placed one on my desk, a tangible connection was made—a bridge between my old life and this new frontier. I picked up the syllabus, my trembling hand tracing the words.

In that moment, my world tightened around me, a constricting grip of self-doubt. Panic bubbled up, threatening to drown out reason. The desire to escape, to retreat from the unfamiliar, was strong. But as my mind raced, I knew I had a choice: to flee or to flourish.

Summoning courage from the depths of my being, I took measured breaths. My grip on the backpack strap gradually loosened, symbolizing my willingness to shed my fears. With deliberate intent, I unzipped the pouch, retrieving my blue pen. It's reassuring weight in my hand anchored me.

Letter by letter, I inked my name onto the syllabus—J-U-D-Y. Each stroke was a declaration that I belonged, that I was capable of navigating this uncharted territory. With every completed letter, my pulse steadied, and my resolve solidified.

By the time my full name, "Judy Serratos," graced the paper, I felt a shift within me. The act of writing my name was a proclamation of self-worth and a testament to my readiness to embrace the unknown. I was not just a passenger on this journey, I was the driver of my destiny.

With newfound clarity, I closed my eyes for a brief moment, grounding myself in the present. The whispers of self-doubt were quieter now, overshadowed by the resounding truth that I was meant to be here. As the professor continued his introduction, I opened my eyes, my gaze meeting his with a newfound sense of purpose.

In that classroom, on that day, I learned a lesson that would guide me through the rest of my college journey and beyond. The road ahead might be uncertain, but by embracing each moment and confronting my fears, I could transform challenges into opportunities. The journey had just begun, and I was ready to embrace it with an open heart and a steadfast spirit.

After each successful year of completing both semesters and earning passing grades in all my college courses, I made it a tradition to celebrate my wins. Year after year, I would save up enough money to visit the bookstore and purchase a CSULB sweater. Each sweater became more than just a piece of clothing, it was a symbol of triumph, a badge of perseverance that I proudly wore.

As I donned those sweaters, I felt a sense of pride and they were reminders of my accomplishments, the sleepless nights, the focused studying, and the moments of doubt conquered. They were more than just garments, they were tangible symbols that I had overcome the challenges that once appeared insurmountable.

Walking through the campus adorned in my CSULB sweater, I experienced a renewed sense of pride and achievement. The doubts that once plagued my mind were now drowned out by the resounding chorus of my successes. The path I had traversed stood as a testament to my unwavering determination, and the sweaters I wore were woven with the threads of my journey, threads representing my growth, resilience, and sense of belonging.

Judy Stella

TWENTY THREE

Growing up in my unpredictable household, where my mother's mood could shift like the wind, studying at home was often an exercise in frustration. With my stack of textbooks beside me, I'd attempt to focus on my schoolwork only to be thwarted by the chaos erupting around me. Desperate for a quiet space to concentrate, I began escaping to the nearby coffee shop after work a couple of times a week. There, nestled in a tranquil corner, I found calm in the hum of conversation and the aroma of freshly brewed coffee.

It was during one of these study sessions that fate intervened in the form of Moses. A regular at the coffee shop, he exuded warmth and familiarity as he greeted fellow patrons and staff. Intrigued by his genuine kindness, I found myself drawn to him, and over time, our brief exchanges evolved into deep conversations about life, learning, and purpose. One evening, he surprised me with a gift—the book *"The Purpose Driven Life"* by Rick Warren—a gesture that touched me deeply.

As our friendship blossomed, Moses became more than just a mentor, he became a steadfast source of support and encouragement. From offering guidance on my studies to providing practical assistance like lending me a printer when mine broke down, his generosity knew no bounds. I'll never forget the day he offered me his spare printer without a moment's hesitation, ensuring that my academic pursuits remained unhindered.

Reflecting on those turbulent years of my youth, I am profoundly grateful for the serendipitous encounter that brought Moses into my life. Over the past two decades, our friendship has endured, a testament to the enduring bond forged through adversity and shared moments of growth. Recently, as we reminisced over dinner, I took the opportunity to express my deepest gratitude to him, acknowledging the profound impact he has had on my life. In Moses, I see not just a friend, but an angel walking among us, a beacon of light guiding me through and navigating the intricate web of life's journey alongside me.

TWENTY FOUR

Months later, around the same time that I was completing my final exams for my first semester of college, a major disruption would occur at home; another explosion of emotions. I was just getting back home from school in the afternoon, and I didn't have a lot of time to get ready and start my shift at work.

My mother was having another explosive episode in which she was yelling at one of my younger sisters. My stepdad was there, acting as a buffer and softening each blow of her actions and berating words towards her. In an effort to protect my sister from her ongoing wrath, I quickly intervened and felt flooded by the emotions of her wrath that would normally be directed at me. Since I was older and hardly ever at home due to my new responsibilities of going to school and work, I had been temporarily saved from her verbal and emotional abuse. Not understanding what would even be the problem that would warrant such a reaction from her. She quickly charged at me and started directing her anger at me. Yelling in my face.

"¿Tú qué chingados te metes, tú no sabes qué está pasando aquí? ¡Como si te pones del lado de él!" (referring to my stepdad).

She became angrier at the thought that I was siding with my stepdad. The reality was I only cared about protecting my sister from her and feared that she would physically hurt my sister in the same ways she had hurt me in the past.

I stayed in the same place, not allowing her to frighten me. I would stand up and protect my sister. My actions enraged my mother further, her rage was full on, and she would not back down. I believe that out of her desperation and loss of control, she began to yell at me again.

"¡Pues esta es mi pinche casa, y aquí se hace lo que yo digo, si no te gusta, lárgate de aquí, no te quiero ver aquí en mi casa! ¡Lárgate!"

I was shocked and frozen in time for what felt like an eternity. It took me a moment to fully understand what had happened. When I was finally able to move, I went quickly to my bedroom, changed into my work uniform, and left for work. Crying on my drive to work, I wasn't sure what my next step would be. My mother had just kicked me out, and I wasn't even sure if I was allowed to return home that night.

In the midst of this turmoil, a glimmer of hope emerged from an unexpected source. In a conversation with my best friend's mother, I timidly voiced my interest in renting her converted garage—a small space with a bedroom, a kitchenette, and a bathroom. With the courage born of desperation, I explained my financial limitations, uncertain if my plea would be met with acceptance.

As I looked down, struggling to contain my emotions, her response came as a lifeline: "Está bien, te rento el cuarto." Relief washed over me as I processed her words. I would have a place to go, a space I could call my own. With renewed determination, I returned home to pack my belongings, my heart heavy with the weight of change.

In the weeks that followed, I felt overwhelmed by the number of tasks I needed to do. I acquired the essentials for my new living space—a bed, a dresser, cooking utensils—all amidst the whirlwind of preparations for my second semester at college. The move was sudden and new, a major shift I had to navigate with resilience and determination.

Despite the challenges, my spirit remained unbroken. As I settled into my new space, I found relief and safety, a haven away from the storms of my past. My best friend's mother and father became a new source of support, offering more than just a room to rent. Their warmth, concern, and care filled the void left by the chaos of home.

Amid the upheaval, Don Felipe's grilled quesadillas became a symbol of comfort and connection, a reminder of the simple joys that could be found amidst life's chaos. And as I moved forward, tackling each semester and overcoming new hurdles, their support remained a steadfast presence, a beacon of hope that had guided me through the storm.

Now, as I reflect on those challenging days, I am filled with a whirlwind of emotions—gratitude, strength, and a profound sense of the transformative power of compassion. The journey from chaos to courage was not an easy one, but it paved the way for a brighter future, one where I could forge my own path and triumph over adversity.

Judy Stella

TWENTY FIVE

My first year of college had been a success, and my new living space had gradually transformed into a place I could truly call home. It had been six months since I moved out and began living on my own, a significant change that required some adjustment. The most immediate difference I noticed was the presence of a quiet and peaceful space to come back to after a long day of school and work. But with this newfound independence came a poignant realization: I no longer had the daily joy of seeing my siblings.

Thoughts of my younger sisters and brother filled my mind regularly. I wondered how they were coping with my absence and if they were alright. I tried to stay involved in their lives as much as I could despite the demands of my studies and job. I made regular visits, bearing treats or pasta from my workplace, and on occasion, I'd pick up my little brother and take him to McDonald's. It was a delicate balancing act, trying to be present in their lives while juggling the responsibilities of school and work.

Another summer came and went, and I returned to school for my sophomore year of college. This time, the campus didn't feel as intimidating; it had become a familiar place. I strolled past the same trees and buildings with a sense of ease. The fall semester began, and everything seemed to be going smoothly until that fateful afternoon.

I was hanging out with my best friend, engaged in light-hearted conversation, when my phone suddenly rang. The caller ID displayed my mother's name, and I quickly motioned to my friend that I needed to take the call. I answered the phone with a casual "Hello," completely unprepared for what I was about to hear.

On the other end of the line, my mother's voice quivered with emotion. She was crying, struggling to find the words to convey the devastating news.

"Judy, se llevaron a los niños, la trabajadora social vino y se llevó a los niños," she managed to say between sobs. "Judy, they took the children, the social worker came and took them away."

In that heart-wrenching moment, my world shattered. I could feel the strength drain from my legs, and I collapsed to the ground. My knees met the rug beneath me, and my upper body slumped forward as if unable to bear the weight of this sudden tragedy. Tears streamed down my cheeks, and I couldn't contain the scream that erupted from deep within me.

"Nooo…" I cried out, the word torn from my soul.

My mother's cries mingled with mine on the phone. The pain and helplessness in her voice only intensified my own anguish. I don't remember how we ended that call or what happened next. All I knew was that my world had been turned upside down in an instant, and the road ahead seemed uncertain and fraught with heartache.

A few weeks before the life-altering call from my mother, I had received another one that had sent shockwaves through my world. That call had been a bleak reminder of the volatile environment my siblings were still living in.

Another explosive episode had unfolded at home, one that had left me feeling helpless and torn between my own aspirations and the safety of my family. During this incident, my mother's anger had reached a terrifying peak, and she had followed through on her threats to harm my sister.

I hadn't been present when it happened, but the details painted a horrifying picture. My mother had used a belt and repeatedly struck my sister's legs. The situation had escalated to the point where my youngest sister had dialed 911, her voice trembling as she informed the police about the unfolding nightmare.

Upon receiving the call, I rushed to my mother's house in the evening, my heart heavy with worry. When I arrived, my sister who had been hurt was already sleeping in my old bed. I sat in the dimly lit living room, trying to process the unthinkable. My mother was absent, having gone out on an errand, leaving behind a heavy silence.

As I perched on the edge of the couch, my head in my hands, a knock at the door shattered the stillness. Two police officers stood on the threshold, their presence a solemn reminder of the gravity of the situation. I confirmed that they had indeed received the distress call. With a heavy heart, I recounted what I knew had transpired, and they nodded in understanding.

However, their duty extended beyond gathering information; they needed to ensure the well-being of my sister. I agreed to their request for a welfare check, and we quietly made our way to what used to be my old bedroom. There, my sister lay sleeping on the left side of the bed, her innocence a stark contrast to the trauma she had endured.

The officers asked me to lift the blanket to reveal the injuries my sister had suffered. With a heavy heart, I complied, exposing the painful lacerations on her legs, inflicted by the belt. The sight was all too familiar. It triggered memories of my own past, of enduring similar pain and welts on my legs.

The officers' faces mirrored my shock and sadness as they surveyed the evidence before them. Turning to me, one of them explained.

"We are required by law to report this incident to child protective services."

Their words hung in the air, a grim reminder of the consequences that would follow such a report. Once again, I nodded, understanding that they were mandated reporters, bound by their duty to protect the welfare of children in such situations.

This chapter is undoubtedly one of the most painful and

challenging to write. Looking back on this experience, hindsight can be a harsh and unforgiving companion. There are moments when I wish I could have rewritten my own history, showed up differently and been there for my sisters and little brother in a more profound way. It's an example of a life event that took nearly two decades to muster the courage to openly share with my therapist.

I remember it vividly. It was during one of my regular weekly therapy sessions, a time when I usually checked in and discussed the ups and downs of life. That day, I walked into the therapist's office feeling strangely okay, and for a quick minute I thought I was going in for a regular check-in session. As the session began, we followed our routine of starting with our usual "How are you, Judy?" But one topic led to another, and suddenly, I found myself sharing the very life-altering event when my siblings were removed from their home and placed in foster care.

My voice trembled, and tears welled up in my eyes. It was as if the memories, emotions, and words were all jumbled up inside me, struggling to find a way out. I felt an overwhelming sense of responsibility, a heavy burden that had weighed on my heart for far too long.

"I feel responsible, I feel like I abandoned my siblings, and the guilt of not living with them at home was unbearable to face," I managed to utter.

With those words, I couldn't hold back the flood of emotions any longer. My head dropped, and I covered my face with my hands, overcome by inconsolable tears. It was at that moment, in the safety of my therapist's office, that I confronted the immense guilt I had carried for years—a guilt stemming from my belief that I had somehow failed to protect my siblings from the abuse and turmoil that continued to plague their lives after I moved out.

This chapter in my life was a painful reckoning, an acknowledgment of the complex emotions and deep-seated guilt that had long been buried. It was a turning point, one that would set me on a path towards understanding and healing, but also a reminder that some wounds take decades to fully reveal themselves.

My therapist offered me a safe space to process and feel my emotions. She stayed quiet, giving me a compassionate nod and reassurance that she was there with me. I felt her presence and support, and as my tears and sobbing gradually subsided, she began to speak with me.

She validated my experience, acknowledging the pain and guilt that had lingered for so long. But she didn't stop there. Through her wisdom, she offered an invaluable insight that would bring a different perspective to what my siblings and I had painfully endured.

She reminded me that although I was an adult in terms of age, I was still a child myself who had endured so much pain and hurt while growing up in the same home. For me to break free and begin to improve my life, and possibly become a role model for my siblings to look up to, it was important that I moved out. It wasn't just a hard choice I hastily made, it was a necessity.

By removing myself from the unhealthy environment that was hurting me as well, I had created a space where I could feel safe, focus on my studies, and work on bettering myself. It was only by improving my own life that I could continue showing up for my siblings in a more meaningful way. My therapist's words provided a glimmer of understanding and self-compassion, slowly chipping away at the heavy burden of guilt I had carried for so long.

TWENTY SIX

The weeks that followed, my siblings' placement in foster care was among the most emotionally taxing I had ever experienced. I felt an overwhelming sense of helplessness, as if I were tethered to the sidelines, unable to do much to change the situation. The social worker assigned to my family's case assured me that the primary goal of child protective services was family reunification. Still, it was a waiting game, and my mother would have to undergo counseling and complete parenting classes before any progress could be made.

During this uncertain period, I reached out to my college counselor, Harrelson, and shared the agonizing details of what had transpired. He lent a sympathetic ear and provided a reassuring perspective. He reminded me that the system was designed to prioritize the reunification of families, emphasizing the importance of my mother's journey towards improvement.

In the months that followed, I threw myself into my studies and work. My grades were decent, but I couldn't quite settle on a major. It was during one of my regular visits to Harrelson, a person who had become both a mentor and a friend, that I shared my desire to pursue a profession where I could make a difference in the lives of others. I contemplated majoring in criminal justice, envisioning a future as a juvenile probation officer or in a similar helping role.

Harrelson, however, introduced me to the field of social work. He encouraged me to delve into its values, ethics, and the diverse roles that social workers play. As I embarked on this journey of self-discovery, I realized that social work aligned perfectly with my passion for helping others.

I began to immerse myself in research, eager to learn about the myriad ways social workers could make a positive impact. Through my own family's experience, I witnessed firsthand the invaluable support provided by our dedicated social worker. She orchestrated a web of services to aid my mother and facilitate the process of family reunification, offering us a glimmer of hope.

It was during this pivotal moment that I decided to major in Social Work. My enthusiasm to acquire knowledge in this field was driven not only by the desire to help others but also by a fervent hope that I could become a resource for my own family. I yearned to guide us through this challenging journey, with the ultimate goal of reuniting my siblings in a much healthier and safer environment than they had ever known.

TWENTY SEVEN

Senior year of college had arrived, and I couldn't have been more excited to start the fall semester. Reuniting with friends and classmates filled me with joy, but there was one person I was particularly eager to see: Dr. Rebecca Lopez, my social policy professor. Her remarkable presence, marked by eloquence and poised confidence, always left a lasting impression. Over time, she had evolved from being my professor to someone I deeply admired and respected.

I relished her lectures, positioning myself in the very front row of her class to ensure I didn't miss a word. There was an air of uniqueness about her. Each time she entered the classroom, her confidence radiated, and when she delved into her subject matter, she did so with eloquence, grace, and dignity. I hung on every word, and when it came to preparing for her midterms and finals, I pushed myself to study harder than ever.

One particular midterm stands out in my memory. Dr. Lopez had cautioned the class to be well-prepared for the essay portion of the exam. I took her words to heart, dedicating an entire week to exhaustive studying. No page of my notes went untouched; I was determined to master the material. On exam day, I poured my heart and soul into answering all four written essay questions and tackling the fifty multiple-choice questions.

A week later, our test scores were returned. Dr. Lopez, holding a towering stack of exams, went through the classroom calling each student's name, personally delivering their scores. Anxiety gnawed at me as I waited for my name to be called. I couldn't wait to see how I had performed.

She was down to her last packet of exams, and I was certain it had to be mine. Slowly, she made her way towards me, her eyes locking onto mine. With a smile that warmed my heart, she extended her arm, my exam in hand, and uttered those words that I would carry with me forever: "Congratulations Miss Serratos, well done."

I looked down at my exam in disbelief. There it was, a perfect score, a testament to my hard work and dedication. When I looked up at Dr. Lopez, her smile seemed to convey not just approval but pride in my achievement. She even gave me a subtle wink before returning to the front of the room.

It's a memory I hold dear, a reminder of how the encouragement and belief of a remarkable teacher can propel us to reach for the stars. What meant the most, though, was that someone noticed my unwavering effort and resilience, even during the times when nobody could fathom the challenges I faced beyond the classroom doors.

TWENTY EIGHT

The new school year had just begun, and as I strolled up to the upper campus, I decided to pay a visit to Harrelson. It was our usual check-in, a chance for me to share my academic progress and life updates. However, this visit took an unexpected turn when he asked me a question that caught me off guard:

"Have you considered applying to graduate school?"

The question hung in the air, and I was momentarily speechless. The idea of graduate school was both intriguing and intimidating. Doubts flooded my mind. Why would I want to pursue further education when my undergraduate years had been challenging enough? The thought of it all felt overwhelming. I turned to Harrelson and asked him to elaborate.

He patiently explained the application process, drawing parallels to my previous experience applying for the bachelor's in social work program. He also highlighted the doors that a master's in social work could open, both in terms of the types of services I could offer and the potential increase in compensation.

With his guidance and encouragement, I decided to take the leap. I began crafting my personal statement, volunteered at my little brother's preschool, and secured letters of recommendation from my volunteer work and Harrelson himself. I applied to just two graduate schools: the University of Southern California and Cal State Long Beach.

In the fall of 2004, I found myself setting foot on the USC campus for the first time. The prestigious University of Southern California left me in awe. The beautiful burgundy brick buildings, expansive green lawns, towering trees shedding their leaves, and students bustling along concrete pathways—it was all breathtaking.

Walking alongside my college buddy, who was also submitting her application, we exchanged incredulous smiles. Turning in our graduate applications at such a renowned institution felt like a dream come true. The excitement bubbled up inside me as I took a deep breath, soaking in the atmosphere.

Overflowing with enthusiasm, I sprinted down the steps and gestured to my friend to accompany me to the university's bookstore. As we entered, my eyes widened at the sight of the two-story emporium of knowledge. Rows upon rows of books invited exploration, but something else seized my attention—a USC sweater, resplendent in crimson and gold.

I dashed over and grabbed one in a size small. She regarded me with a blend of surprise and amusement.

"Judy, you're crazy! You don't even know if you'll get accepted." I met her gaze with an even wider smile and a heart brimming with hope. With that USC sweater in my possession, I felt a hint of the incredible journey ahead.

The USC sweater wasn't merely an item of clothing; it was a pledge. A symbol of my dreams crystallizing. It served as evidence of the enchantment that transpires when you dare to dream and labor diligently to manifest those dreams. It was a reminder that our dreams, regardless of their enormity, are attainable. The tiniest steps can lead to the loftiest summits, and I was prepared to ascend. This sweater epitomized the might of self-belief.

TWENTY NINE

The following several weeks, I threw myself into my studies, diligently attending all my courses and completing my internship hours. Just before the holidays, my mom called to deliver the uplifting news that she had successfully fulfilled all the requirements set by the Children's Court for family reunification. My sisters and little brother would be allowed to come back home.

I was overjoyed, my heart bursting with happiness. The sense of optimism washed over me, and I eagerly anticipated our reunion. I held onto the hope that our lives would continue to improve, like a phoenix rising from the ashes.

Inspired and full of courage, I broached the idea with my mom of us moving to a new apartment together. This way, we could provide support in this new chapter of our lives. With my graduate school acceptance still uncertain, I wasn't sure what demands and time commitments lay ahead but being close to my siblings and supporting my mom financially felt like the right step. I had missed them immensely.

I scoured the rental market, hoping to find the perfect place. However, rents were high, and suitable options were limited. I yearned for a nicer place in a quiet neighborhood, an apartment that could serve as the backdrop for our fresh start.

After weeks of relentless searching, I stumbled upon an apartment in the nicer part of Hawthorne. This unit was managed by a professional property management company, and as I soon discovered their process involved a complete rental application, a credit check, and upfront payments of the full deposit and the first month's rent, the reality set in: I had never navigated such a complex rental process before. Though it felt stressful and overwhelming, I summoned my courage and called the property management office to schedule a showing that same afternoon.

I raced up the stairs to the second floor, anxious not to be late for my appointment to view the apartment. My heart pounded as I approached the open door. George, a tall, older man with glasses, welcomed me inside. I entered with caution, a mix of nerves and hope swirling within me. Adrenaline surged as I crossed into what I silently prayed would be our new family home.

At twenty-one years old, I was already juggling a multitude of responsibilities. I questioned how I would manage should this apartment become ours. However, on that afternoon, I decided to seize an opportunity. During the showing, I recognized a chance to share our family's story with George, the property manager. With my neck craned to make eye contact with this towering man, I finally found my voice.

"George," I began, my words emerging with hesitation, "this apartment is precisely what our family needs. We've been separated for several months, but now we have the chance to reunite, to bring my siblings back home just in time for Christmas. I know the rent and the required deposit, and I promise we'll never be late with it. I'll take full responsibility for my family. We just need this one chance, please."

My eyes welled up, and for a moment, I felt exposed and vulnerable. But it was the most honest plea I could make, and the only words I had.

George gazed at me, his own eyes glistening with tears, and then he smiled.

"Alright," he said, "let's see what I can do."

My words seemed to touch his heart as I told him about our imminent reunification and my desperate need for a fresh start. I reassured him that I would shoulder all the responsibilities, signing the lease contract under my name and utilizing my financial aid money to cover all the initial costs. It was a leap of faith, a significant step toward securing a stable and comfortable home for my family and for myself in this new chapter of our lives.

Judy Stella

THIRTY

The property manager's belief in me felt like a ray of sunshine breaking through the clouds. He saw a young woman, seemingly mature beyond her years, and he was genuinely happy to support our family in this new chapter of our lives. The relief I felt was immeasurable.

I couldn't wait to bring my mom and siblings to see the apartment. It was a two-bedroom space, complete with its own bathroom, a spacious living room, and a kitchen with a small dining area. As you walked in, the apartment greeted you with the fresh scent of paint. The walls were clean and freshly painted, the dark wooden cabinets and new carpet gave the place an air of promise. It was as if we had hit the jackpot; this was one of the nicest living spaces our family had ever known.

My excitement was undeniable. This was a chance for a fresh start, a new beginning. With me handling the finances and paperwork, my mother only needed to pack lightly and ensure my siblings had what they needed for their return home. It brought her immense relief and marked a significant step toward stability for our family.

Over the next two weeks, we embarked on the journey of moving into our new apartment. I brought in all of my furniture, kitchen appliances, and my cherished books. My mom arranged her bedroom furniture and made sure my siblings had their clothes and essentials for their personal care and schooling.

In the following weeks after our move, we slowly fell into a new rhythm and became reacquainted with living together. Coordinating morning bathroom routines in our one-bathroom apartment became quite the task, as all my sisters and I were now getting ready for school at the same time.

These days were special for me. I enjoyed the daily interactions with my sisters, especially witnessing them navigate their teenage years. They'd often ask for my fashion advice or if they could borrow my hair and makeup products. I was the big sister, and I cherished the chance to nurture our sibling bonds and be a part of their lives.

My biggest desire was to continue to be available for my sisters, continue to support them, and be the positive role model for them that comes with being the oldest sister. Their adolescence was a unique time, filled with the excitement of dating and hanging out with friends. I had the opportunity to see my sisters happy, building relationships with their peers, and experiencing all the typical activities of growing up.

I cherish those unforgettable moments spent with my little brother. Each afternoon after school, I'd walk through the door and find him in the living room surrounded by his toys. As soon as he saw me, a radiant smile would light up his face, revealing his small silver teeth and the sparkle in his eyes. Coming home to that warm and sweet smile was a daily joy that filled my heart with happiness.

On the days when I didn't have to rush off to work right after school, I made sure to slow down and invite my little brother to join me in the kitchen for a snack. We'd sit at our small wooden dining table, and I'd make a peanut butter and jelly sandwich or warm leftovers from Mom's cooking the night before. As we faced each other, I listened attentively to the stories he shared. One conversation during this time stood out to me. He spoke with such enthusiasm about his vision and dream of growing up to start his own business and become a millionaire. I couldn't help but smile and nod, hoping that he felt seen and that his big sister was supportive and encouraging of his dreams. It was during these moments that I realized the importance of being a positive influence on my siblings, nurturing their ambitions and helping them believe that they could achieve anything.

The joy of having everyone together was indescribable. Seeing my mom every day was a comfort. I knew the past several months had been incredibly difficult and stressful for her. Finally, we were all living under the same roof. Despite our busy schedules, we managed to find quiet moments to catch up and share our experiences. I particularly relished my mom's home-cooked meals. They were a source of support for me, as I rarely had time to sit down to a proper meal due to my hectic schedule. While my mom might not have fully understood everything I was studying and doing during my internship, she would often step into my room, offering me a snack and words of encouragement when she found me awake late at night studying for exams.

"Así, hija, sigue estudiando, síguele echando ganas. Que todo sacrificio vale la pena," she would say, reminding me that all the sacrifices were worthwhile.

As I write these words today, reflecting on my life as a mother of two at the age of forty, I realize in hindsight that there are many things I would have done differently. I long to have been more present, more considerate in checking in with my siblings, understanding how they coped with the profound changes and emotions tied to our reunions after months of separation. Each time I revisit this chapter of our lives, tears well up, aching for the pain we all endured, especially my younger siblings, whose feelings and thoughts remained uncertain to me. Today, I offer myself grace and self-compassion, finding solace in the knowledge that I genuinely did my best to support them. My deepest hope is that they always feel my love, unwavering support, and sincere desire for their well-being.

THIRTY ONE

As my life was taking shape in various ways, personal changes were taking place too. I remember one crisp morning during a short break between classes, I decided to step out for some fresh air. There, serendipitously, I crossed paths with an old friend from high school, Erick.

We had shared a group of friends back in our senior year of high school, and though our encounters had been limited to brief moments on campus or at weekend college parties, I was thrilled to see a familiar face. I began to share the whirlwind of my life, juggling midterm papers, the demands of my internship, and the excitement of applying to graduate school. It felt like a breath of fresh air amidst the recent turmoil in my family.

However, there was an undercurrent, something I couldn't ignore. As we spoke, I couldn't help but notice the handsome transformation Erick had undergone. For the first time in the many years since I had known him, I truly saw his big smile and perfectly aligned teeth. His eyes held a special sparkle every time he grinned, and I found solace in the softness of his spoken words. Instantly, an attraction blossomed—a crush, accompanied by the fluttering of butterflies in my stomach, signaling the onset of feelings I couldn't ignore.

From that day forward, I eagerly anticipated every crossing of our paths on campus or the prospect of hanging out, even if only for a few minutes. Messages were exchanged, and in the midst of our last semester of college, juggling midterms and work, we managed to steal a few moments together. Occasionally, amidst our busy days, we found weekends or precious hours between classes to hang out and chat.

One memorable weekend, we decided on the beach, bringing our rollerblades to traverse The Strand at Manhattan Beach. I vividly remember a moment of panic as we zoomed down a slope. Unfamiliar with the brakes, I instinctively clung to Erick, and together we tumbled into a rose bush. Laughter erupted, creating a shared joke that epitomized our ability to find humor in the unexpected. To this day, we reminisce about that incident, laughing as Erick teases me about purposely pushing him into the rose bush.

In those enjoyable moments on the sandy shores, the world outside our connection seemed to fade away. The rhythm of our barefoot runs, the shared laughter, and the hushed conversations painted a vibrant picture, making the stresses of family and school take a backseat. The beach became our sanctuary, a place where time slowed, and we could revel in the simplicity of our togetherness. The whispers of the ocean seemed to echo the unspoken sentiments growing between us.

As the weeks unfolded, my feelings for Erick deepened, transcending the initial flutter of butterflies. I found myself envisioning our relationship as something more profound than two young adults navigating college dating. The prospect of becoming a couple, taking on the title of his girlfriend, started to materialize in my thoughts. The evolution of our connection became a quiet certainty, a bond that extended beyond the confines of casual companionship.

Let me share another tale that some would say solidified the idea that Erick and I were destined to be together. Now, if you were to ask him about it today, he'd probably laugh and offer a completely different perspective from my version of the story. Here's how it unfolded.

Back when we were high school seniors, Erick and I shared the same group of friends. Our hangout spot during lunch was a simple bench by Nyman Hall. Around this time, Erick had made the decision to become a vegetarian. When some of our peers teased him for his dietary choice, I would step in, inviting him to join me at the snack bar.

Together, we'd order two bean and cheese burritos and an orange juice, my small way of supporting his new diet. Little did I know this routine was laying the groundwork for something more in the future.

Erick gradually became my new lunch buddy, and looking back, he was one of those cool guy friends I genuinely enjoyed spending time with. One day, during our usual lunch gathering, I realized Erick was nowhere to be found. Concerned, I asked our friend Sergio if he'd seen Erick, and he mentioned that Erick was at school, working on an assignment in Mr. Anderson's class during lunch.

Grateful for the update, I headed to the snack bar, ordered our usual lunches, and made my way to the classroom where Erick was. With a smile, I greeted him and offered to keep him company while he finished his assignment. This simple act of friendship would later be interpreted in vastly different ways.

Reflecting on this memory, I see it as a time when I cared for Erick as a friend, long before any romantic or physical attraction emerged. It was a genuine, platonic interest in a cool friend. However, Erick, being the charming storyteller he is, likes to recount it as evidence that I always had an interest in him, a supposed obsession from way back in the day. Today, we laugh and joke about these differing perspectives, and it's moments like these that showcase his sense of humor—one of the many reasons I fell head over heels for him.

Our friendship blossomed into a romantic love, a journey that, like many others, unraveled the complexities of intimacy and brought forth past pains. The wounds of our childhoods, coupled with limited communication and problem-solving skills, emerged as challenges we had to confront together.

In the early months of our time dating, Erick and I faced these difficulties head-on. Unhealthy communication patterns and limited problem-solving abilities surfaced, exemplified by my struggle with expressing my feelings clearly and directly. The pivotal moment, the first significant hurdle in our relationship, occurred when Erick expressed hesitancy about moving our dating status to boyfriend and girlfriend. It was a heartbreaking revelation, leaving me silent and teary-eyed, grappling with the pain of feeling not enough and rejected.

In the aftermath, days passed without communication. I lacked the emotional maturity and insight to navigate the situation effectively. Yet, the longing for Erick's company persisted, and I found myself reaching out to him after a few days or weeks, resuming our time together. A part of me clung to the hope that he would change his stance, and eventually, we did become an official couple. Our relationship unfolded organically, progressing through the phases of exclusivity, engagement, marriage, and starting a family.

As the years passed, Erick and I embarked on our individual and shared healing journeys. We revisited childhood wounds, faced traumas, and grappled with the absence of healthy coping skills needed for an optimal relationship. Our first-generation status added another layer, as the expectations and drive to succeed, rooted in honoring our parents' sacrifices, influenced our perspectives.

Erick envisioned himself as a successful entrepreneur, viewing serious relationships as potential distractions. His perception of love and marriage was tainted by the pain and loss from his parents' divorce when he was twelve. For a long time, he held onto the belief that he never wanted to get married.

On my end, the wounds of abandonment and feelings of inadequacy stemmed from my parents' separation when I was only three years old. The absence of a father's love and nurturance in my life left deep traces.

Navigating these challenges without the proper tools and support was extremely difficult and we did our best as a young couple. Eventually, our personal growth journeys guided us towards new insights and a promising future. We read books, listened to podcasts, sought individual and couples therapy, and learned to communicate and understand each other better. In almost twenty years together, we've built a strong foundation, supporting each other's growth and dreams, and remaining committed to our marriage. I am grateful for the journey, proud of the individuals we've become, and hopeful that God will grant us a long and blessed life together.

THIRTY TWO

Fate stepped in once more at a crucial juncture in my life. On a bustling Sunday morning, amid the lively brunch hour, an elderly gentleman entered the restaurant, expressing a desire to occupy my section. Though unfamiliar to me, I eagerly approached his booth, ready to offer hospitality. He asked for a hot tea with honey, and as I guided him to the brunch station, I assured him of my readiness to assist further. In response, he beamed, delivering the most radiant smile I had ever encountered, expressing gratitude for my kindness.

The following week held a delightful surprise as Mr. Charles Saullo, now a familiar face, returned. He expressed his enjoyment of the brunch, praising my service. For the next two years, he continued to make a weekly journey from Inglewood to Redondo Beach, arriving by bus to savor hot tea, waffles, and fresh fruit. Our new friendship flourished, and within it, I discovered not just his favorite tea but also cherished our heartfelt conversations.

Mr. Saullo became a constant in my life. His genuine interest in my educational journey and encouragement became a comforting presence. His calm demeanor acted as an anchor during a tumultuous time. As I pursued my master's degree at USC, he celebrated my achievements with a warmth akin to a proud grandparent. His support was boundless, and his wisdom served as a well of inspiration.

Despite the strong connection we shared, there were facets of Mr. Saullo's life he chose to keep private. When inquiring about his family, he politely declined, stating it was too painful to discuss. I respected his wishes and never broached the topic again. Our Sundays continued with joyous greetings and warm welcomes.

As my USC graduation approached, Mr. Saullo's pride for me was palpable. Opening the graduation card he gifted me filled me with overwhelming emotion, a sense of accomplishment, and the knowledge that I had made him proud. His card became a cherished keepsake, a source of encouragement during uncertain times.

Post-graduation, I left the restaurant to embark on the next chapter of my life. Excitement for new opportunities coexisted with the knowledge that I would miss our weekly encounters. We exchanged contact information, ensuring our connection would continue outside the restaurant. Regular calls ensued, providing updates on our lives.

One day, while driving home, thoughts of Mr. Saullo prompted me to call him. Discovering he was at the local library, I made a spontaneous decision to meet him. Hours were spent sharing stories, reminiscing about our brunches, and catching up. Plans were made to revisit the restaurant as guests, but fate had other plans.

Then came the day when worry tightened its grip around my heart. Multiple attempts to reach Mr. Saullo went unanswered, and a chilling realization set in when I learned his number was no longer in service. Fearful for his well-being, I raced to the senior assisted living center where he resided, only to be met with devastating news: he had passed away two weeks prior, alone and without any known family or friends.

The guilt of not being there for him in his final days hung heavy on my soul. Determined to honor his memory, I worked tirelessly to ensure he received a proper farewell. Discovering that he was a veteran, the hospital assured me that assistance would be provided for a dignified service and burial.

On the day of his funeral, I found myself driving to Covina Hills Forest Lawn with a mix of nervousness and sorrow. With a small bouquet of white flowers, I entered the chapel and was greeted by the chaplain. His inquiry about other attendees brought forth the painful reality that I was the sole witness to bid farewell to Mr. Saullo.

As the chaplain spoke eloquently, acknowledging the cyclical nature of life and death, I sat in solitude, tears streaming down my cheeks. When invited to share, I stood before an empty room and recounted our friendship—the brunches, the conversations, and the profound impact he had on my life. In that solemn moment, I acknowledged the void his absence left, yet celebrated the richness he brought to my world.

Despite the sorrow, the chaplain encouraged me to share the beauty of our friendship. Through teary eyes, I shared our story, emphasizing his impact on my life. Gratitude flowed for his kind heart, the encouragement he provided, and the self-worth he instilled in me during trying times. In that quiet chapel, I realized the depth of our connection and how one man's kindness had made a profound impact in my life.

"Today, I stand alone, but not without love for Mr. Saullo. His impact on my life is immeasurable. His gentle demeanor and genuine kindness shaped the person I am today. His words were a lifeline, reminding me of my worthiness even in the darkest moments."

I took a deep breath, finding solace in the memories we shared.

"I carry his graduation card with me, a constant reminder of his belief in me. In his absence, I am grateful for the privilege of being here today, ensuring that he is not forgotten. Mr. Saullo may have left this world quietly, but his presence will forever resonate in my heart."

In that chapel, I whispered my final goodbye to a friend whose presence had illuminated my path, imprinting an everlasting legacy I now affectionately call "The Saullo Effect." His memory, a reservoir of inspiration and gratitude, propels me towards a higher purpose—a pursuit of kindness, authentic connections, and an understanding of the profound influence one soul can have over another.

As I carry his memory forward, I am constantly reminded of the moments when hope seemed elusive and discouragement loomed, underscoring once more the transformative power of others showing up, extending their kindness, and bestowing upon us the beautiful gift of human connection.

Judy Stella

THIRTY THREE

I'd like to share the first time I saw my mother as a whole and separate human being apart from me. It was during an afternoon reunion in which I had invited my mother to lunch at her favorite restaurant. We were enjoying an appetizer, with her favorite salad and breadsticks. I remember how she was so excited to be together, she was smiling, sitting up straight with a warmth and softness in her eyes. I realized at that moment how happy she was that I had invited her to have lunch and for the opportunity to be together, evident by her gently reaching across the table to touch my hand. I felt uncomfortable by her touching gesture.

My mom looked at me, saying my name first until I looked up at her and finally our eyes made contact.

"I know I wasn't the perfect mother; I recognize that I've made a lot of mistakes while raising you and your siblings." She paused, and then said, "But I also don't think I was this horrible mother."

I paused. I took several deep breaths before opening my mouth to say something. Looking at my mother, it felt as if this exact moment froze in time just enough to really take in her message.

This exact moment, when I paused and looked at my mother, was the very first time I recognized that my mother was a human being worthy of being listened to, and even if our realities differed vastly, my mother's story was just as valid and significant as mine. A newfound compassion was felt for my mother, many thoughts floated across inside my mind, and I asked myself, if she was comparing my childhood and her efforts to be the best mother to me to her own childhood. She most likely landed on her conclusion that she was not a horrible mother from there.

I struggled with facing a painful question: how much worse and painful of a reality was my mother's childhood and life in comparison to mine? Although in recent years I have learned more intimate details of her upbringing and life experiences, I am overwhelmed with this newfound compassion and grace for my mother.

THIRTY FOUR

On a March evening in 2020, I extended an invitation to my mother, offering to pick her up after work and join me for dinner. With a sense of nostalgia, we found ourselves at El Cerro Verde, a restaurant that echoed the flavors of cherished memories from my childhood. Recollections flooded my mind, taking me back to weekends when my mother would order pupusas and plátanos fritos from a church nearby. Those moments around the dining table, savoring a delicious meal, left a lasting imprint on my heart, influencing my choice of venue for this intimate gathering.

As we sat down for dinner, the atmosphere was filled with a medley of emotions. We delved into familiar topics, discussing the well-being of my kids and my experiences in our family business. Yet, the air shifted when my mother, after twenty-six years, broached a subject that had long been buried—the time I had disclosed the physical and sexual abuse that had occurred.

A deep breath hung in the air as I grappled with the uncertainty of the conversation's direction. I listened intently, realizing that my mother intended to share her recent experiences processing this painful incident in her individual therapy. Her words unfolded a narrative of regret, acknowledging the red flags she had missed, and the poor handling of the situation. Another deep breath, and I shared my own journey through therapy, expressing my decision to no longer address the perpetrator as my dad, and my desire to distance myself from him at family events.

In the weighty silence that followed, tears flowed freely. My mother gently held my left hand, her own eyes brimming with emotion.

"Pero no llores, Judy," she whispered.

"No, mami, déjame llorar, que es bueno llorar para sacar todo esto que siento por dentro," I insisted. (No, Mom, let me cry. It's good to cry to release all that I feel inside.)

We sat in what felt like an eternity, tears tracing a path down our cheeks. Brief moments of eye contact punctuated the shared sorrow, and, with a napkin, I wiped away my own tears. Then, in a gesture of comfort, my mother covered my right arm with her hand, squeezing gently but refusing to let go. Her eyes locked onto mine, and with a steady and assured voice.

"Tú eres una luchona, y me siento muy orgullosa de ti. Yo te quiero mucho y cuentas con mi apoyo incondicionalmente." she declared. (You're a fighter, and I'm very proud of you. I love you very much, and you have my unconditional support.)

Her words were a salve, a tsunami of healing waves washing over the pain of my inner child. For years, all I had yearned for was my mother's acknowledgment, acceptance, and pride. In that moment, I felt seen, understood, and embraced with unwavering support, a profound reassurance that mended the deepest wounds of my soul.

On that very evening, I drove my mother home. As we lingered in my car exchanging goodbyes, I found myself pausing once more, drawing in a deep breath. In that moment, I made a decision—a choice that I've come to regard as pivotal. With sincerity, I enveloped my mother in a heartfelt embrace, planting a tender kiss on her cheek. "Te quiero, mamá", I whispered softly, the words slipping from my lips. Yet, the overwhelming surge of emotion that flooded through me, reaching the depths of my being, remains indescribable to this day. No words, no matter how carefully crafted, could ever capture its essence adequately. But I know, beyond any doubt, that it was felt—by both her and me.

A Letter to My Mother

Dearest Mother,

As I reflect on the journey we've shared, I am moved by the myriad of experiences that have shaped us. Together, we've weathered storms of pain and regret, and it's only now that the once scattered puzzle pieces of our lives are beginning to form a beautiful beginning. With this newfound understanding, I sincerely apologize for those moments when I couldn't grasp the situation and unfairly judged things beyond my understanding.

Today, I look at you and our shared experiences through a lens of compassion and healing. Mom, I want you to know that you were not a horrible mother; there were many things you did exceptionally well. Regrettably, we found ourselves ensnared in the painful web of generational trauma, a burden that neither of us deserved to carry. You endured a depth of pain and suffering greater than I could fathom, and I wish we hadn't had to navigate through such challenging moments.

The undeniable truth is that the strength and resilience I possess today, the essence of a 'luchona', is a testament to the unwavering example you set. I acknowledge and appreciate the sacrifices you made for me.

I want to express my heartfelt apologies for the pain and suffering you endured while desperately trying to stay afloat and be a mother to me. Now, as a mother myself, I can empathize with the challenges you faced, clinging to the last thread of stability while being responsible for another life.

I thank God for the miracle of healing that has blessed our relationship. May this newfound understanding be a source of compassion and grace that continues to envelop us. My prayer for you is that you always feel loved and cherished, knowing that I have let go of any lingering resentments. Mom, I love you deeply, and my greatest hope is that God grants you a long and fulfilling life. If the beginning of our journey was fraught with challenges, I embrace the opportunity for a healthy, loving, and nurturing relationship in this next chapter of our lives.

You are the biggest miracle in my life, and I am grateful for this second chance to experience a full circle of love and understanding with you. I love you, Mom.

With all my love,
Your Daughter, Judy

THIRTY FIVE

Embarking on the journey of motherhood has been one of the most profound and transformative life experiences, shaping not only my life but also the lives of the precious souls I brought into this world. It is a responsibility that I hold dear, recognizing it as the most significant contribution I have made during my existence on this Earth. While I cherish other dreams and aspirations, the role of a mother has become a cornerstone, a profound identity that intertwines with the very fabric of my being.

Motherhood, for me, became an opportunity to reconnect with my own inner child—a chance to navigate the delicate terrain of healing my childhood wounds while guiding my own children through the labyrinth of life. It demanded that I confront the shadows of my past, acknowledging and working to heal generational trauma. In the process, I found myself on an emotional rollercoaster, learning to regulate my own central nervous system in the hopes of breaking free from the chains of dysfunctional family cycles.

Like many parents, I harbored dreams of providing my children with more than just material comforts. My aspirations extended far beyond the visible, rooted in a profound desire to offer them a childhood that contrasted with my own. As you, dear reader, have journeyed through my story, you've gained insights into the challenges of my own upbringing, insights that fuel my daily motivation to be present for my children no matter how arduous parenthood may feel at times.

Surviving the echoes of my past was not enough; I aimed for

thriving. I endeavored to be a mother who transcended the limitations of old wounds, fostering a well-rounded sense of purpose in the lives of my children. It was imperative that I break the cycles and meet their needs—physically, emotionally, and spiritually.

Even before my children took their first breaths, I committed to seeking therapy with a mental health professional. I embarked on a journey of self-healing, fully aware that the process would be ongoing. Over the years, I devoured books on parenting, listened to countless podcast episodes, and attended conferences and workshops. My thirst for knowledge stemmed not only from a personal quest for growth but also from a deep understanding of how ignorance and a lack of self-awareness could perpetuate generational trauma.

Acknowledging my humanity, I've made mistakes along this motherhood journey. Yet, I've learned the art of self-compassion and grace. Repairing became a powerful tool, listening to my children's needs a sacred practice, and validating their emotions a foundation to our connection. My priority was clear: to cultivate a secure attachment and provide a home with a strong foundation wrapped around love and nurturance.

Motherhood became a lens through which I gained empathy for my own mother. Struggling with postpartum depression, I sought therapy during the darkest times, holding two truths simultaneously— my painful childhood reality and a newfound compassion for my mother's own history of trauma. It was a delicate dance between acknowledging the past and understanding the complexities that shaped her journey.

Rejecting the notion of a selfless, sacrificial motherhood, I chose intentionality in decision-making for our family. With my husband, we defined parameters aligned with our core values, leaving room for flexibility and ongoing evaluation. The essence was to ensure that our children always felt connected, understood, and accepted; their self-worth would be unquestionable.

Leading with intention meant being present and conscious, pouring myself into motherhood without compromising my well-being. Through ebbs and flows, small acts of self-care became instrumental in ensuring that my children experienced a loving mother capable of extending comfort and compassion. The courage to face motherhood became synonymous with the bravery required to raise both my children and my inner child simultaneously—a commitment rooted in unconditional love and belonging.

A Letter to My Children

To My Beloved Children,

You are my constant inspiration, the reason I wake up each day determined to become the best version of myself. Your presence in my life encourages me to be a kinder, more compassionate person and to stay connected with my emotions.

I humbly ask for your forgiveness for the times I have fallen short, not responding with the kindness and gentleness you deserve. I recognize my mistakes, and I want you to know that any shortcomings on my part have nothing to do with your inherent value and the love you deserve.

I won't offer a list of reasons or justifications because I never want you to feel that my actions were justified. Instead, I strive each day to be a better mother to you. My greatest wish, as I pray to God daily, is for the gift of a long life so that I can continue to be brave and grow as your mother.

My love for you is immeasurable, my beautiful love bugs. Regardless of what challenges life brings our way, always remember how significant and special you are to me. May the warmth of love forever embrace you, and may you never doubt the depth of my love for you.

With all my love,
Mom

THIRTY SIX

Let's rewind to an earlier chapter in my memoir, where I first introduced you to my dear friend Auggie. Remember him? Fast forward to the moment I received a message that would change the course of my life.

It was October 8th, 2022, when Enrique, an old busser from my Marie Callender's days, reached out to me on Facebook. The news he delivered struck me with a mix of shock and sorrow—our dear friend Auggie was in the hospital. According to Enrique, Auggie had lost his eyesight, and his leg had been amputated due to complications with diabetes. The revelation explained the years of unanswered messages I had sent him.

Fueled by concern and a deep desire to reconnect, I embarked on a mission to find Auggie. I scoured through old belongings, searching for a phone that might still carry his home phone number. With every digit I dialed, my heart raced, praying for a lifeline to information about my friend. A glimmer of hope emerged when Auggie's son answered the call, confirming his struggles with health issues and his transfer to a nursing facility in Orange County.

The next day, I made the hour-long drive to visit Auggie, unsure of what I would find. As I entered his room, the nurse informed me that he was undergoing physical therapy. I requested a moment to say hello and assured her I would wait in the common area. The curtain was drawn halfway, revealing Auggie sitting propped up, a shadow of the vibrant soul I once knew. His frailty and the toll of his health battles weighed heavily on my heart, and tears welled up as I greeted him.

"Hola, Auggie, soy Judy," I uttered with a shaky voice. His gaze met mine, and confusion clouded his eyes.

"Judy?" he whispered.

Reassuringly, I repeated, "Sí, Auggie, soy Judy, de Marie Callender's."

Emotions overwhelmed us, and we embraced, tears streaming down both our faces. I couldn't shake the fear that he might not remember me, but as I spoke my name and our shared history, recognition dawned on his face, and we wept together.

We retreated to an outdoor patio, hand in hand, and our conversation unfolded. Auggie shared the hardships of the past year, expressing a desire to end his life due to the challenges he faced. My heart ached, but I embraced the role of a compassionate listener, offering solace and understanding.

"I'm here, Auggie. I promise I won't leave you," I vowed, holding space for his pain.

As we spoke for hours, our conversation delved into personal stories—his journey from Mexico to the U.S., my family, and the profound impact he had on my life. It was a poignant moment when I realized that Auggie hailed from the same town as my father.

"Auggie, I think my father sent you to me so that you could be my father on this Earth," I confessed, tightening my grip on his hand.

His eyes sparkled with pride as he commended the woman and mother I had become. Gratitude swelled within me, but an unspoken truth lingered—I needed to lay bare my heart's deepest sentiments.

"Diosito sent you to show me a father's love. You believed in me, nurtured me, and guided me through my darkest times," I confessed, tears flowing freely. Auggie returned my sentiment, affirming his love and pride in me.

As the afternoon waned, fatigue etched across Auggie's face.

I helped him settle back into his room, assisted with lunch, and offered my contact information to the nurse, pledging my commitment to be there for Auggie.

"Yes, you can call her. She is my daughter, and I love her very much," he asserted in a moment of clarity.

Those were the last words Auggie spoke to me. Days later, a somber call delivered the news of his passing. The ache of longing to see him again mixed with the understanding that his health battles had deprived him of the life he deserved. Regret surfaced for not being by his side in his last moments, but I clung to the promise to honor his love.

My beloved Auggie, my affection and love for you runs deep. Not a single day passes without you crossing my thoughts. Your farewell words remain engraved in my heart, motivating me to embody the love you graciously shared. I aspire to be a compassionate and nurturing person, hoping to make you proud each day. May my deeds, expressions, and the love I share with others mirror the wonderful legacy you left behind and the profound influence you had on my life.

Judy Stella

THIRTY SEVEN

My dad passed away when I was just eight years old, leaving a void in my heart that I didn't fully understand for many years. It took me a long time—thirty years, to be exact—to come to terms with his death and allow myself to grieve.

Growing up, I had convinced myself that I shouldn't feel his loss deeply because I didn't have any vivid memories with him. My parents had separated when I was three years old, and since then, my dad had been absent from my life. I reasoned that if I didn't have many memories to hold onto, then I didn't have the right to mourn him.

But in March 2021, everything changed. It was a month that would forever alter the course of my life. Something within me shifted, and I decided to confront the pain and sadness I had been suppressing all those years. I finally allowed myself to grieve, to acknowledge the void his absence had left in my life.

As I delved into the depths of my emotions, I realized that I carried a deep yearning for my father's love. Despite the lack of memories, I discovered that I held so much love for him in my heart. I couldn't deny the connection we shared, even if it was cut short and overshadowed by the circumstances of our separation.

The weight of his absence became evident as I began to unravel my emotions. It affected me in ways I hadn't fully grasped before. I longed for the moments we could have had, the experiences we could have shared together. I yearned for a different life, one where our bond wasn't severed at such a young age.

Allowing myself to grieve and acknowledge these feelings was a cathartic experience. It was as if I was finally granting myself permission to mourn, to honor the memory of my dad, and to confront the impact of his absence on my life. The pain and sadness were overwhelming at times, but through the tears, I found healing.

I realized that it's never too late to grieve, to mourn the loss of someone who played a significant role in my life. It doesn't matter if the memories are few or if the time we spent together was brief. The love I hold for them is genuine, and the pain of their absence is entirely valid.

So, here I am, thirty years later, finally giving myself the chance to grieve my dad's passing. I carry his memory in my heart, knowing that the love I have for him will always be a part of me. And as I move forward, I strive to live a life that would make him proud, embracing the lessons I've learned from his absence, and cherishing the connections I have with those who are still by my side.

THIRTY EIGHT

In the Spring of 2021, a gentle breeze of change drifted through my life, sparking a newfound curiosity and a yearning to connect with the roots of my family. This transformative journey began to unfold as I honored the whispers of my intuition, guiding me towards a deeper understanding of my biological father. It was during this season of renewal that I took the courageous step of reaching out to my mother, hoping to unveil more about the elusive figure who had remained a mystery throughout my existence.

Despite my mother's sincere efforts, the details she could provide were limited, leaving me with only fragments of information about my father. The turning point occurred on a memorable evening, March 6th, 2021, when my husband and I visited his brother and family.

Over dinner, my brother-in-law shared his experience of discovering long-lost family members through an online ancestry resource. Intrigued by the possibility, we embarked on our own journey to unearth the secrets of my father's lineage.

The path ahead was not without obstacles. Armed with only his full name and place of birth, we faced a daunting challenge in our search. Yet, a moment of inspiration struck as I pondered the years, attempting to deduce the approximate time of his passing. With a sense of hopeful anticipation we keyed in the year '1991', and to our astonishment, a successful search result materialized on the computer screen. Fueled by this discovery, I ventured online to request a death certificate, uncertain if the information would indeed lead me to my father.

Several weeks later, on a serene morning, May 17th, 2021, the gentle knock of a UPS delivery man heralded a momentous event. As I signed a large envelope, he wished me a good day, unaware of the profound emotions concealed within. Behind closed doors, I carefully tore open the envelope, revealing the dark blue border that signified my father's death certificate. My trembling hands navigated the document, verifying each detail against the knowledge I had carried for years.

"This is him, my father," I whispered, tears welling up in my eyes. Overwhelmed by a surge of emotions, I retreated to our guestroom, closing the door behind me as a tidal wave of feelings threatened to engulf me. Kneeling on the floor, my legs gave way, and a profound lamentation emerged from deep within. It was an unrestrained outpouring of grief and mourning, a torrent of emotions I had suppressed for almost three decades. The memories of my mother's announcement, the numbness I felt, and the hesitant refusal to partake in the rituals of his passing all flooded back, now finding expression in this poignant moment of realization.

A Letter to My Father

To My Beloved Father,

As I pen these words, I can't help but marvel at the sheer miracle of finding you and being able to visit the sacred ground where you lay to rest. My heart overflows with emotion, and I sense, with a profound certainty, that your influence has always been a guiding light in my life.

For years, a numbness and emptiness gripped me whenever I gazed at the few photos we shared during my baptism. It wasn't until I held tangible proof of your departure in my hands that the buried emotions within me began to surface. The pain of admitting how profoundly your absence affected me was both heart-wrenching and necessary.

Now, I understand more deeply than ever how much I truly needed you. The longing for a father's love and affection surfaced within me for the first time, and I opened my heart to connect with the love residing in my heart for you. In a somewhat surreal turn of events, as I traveled great distances to honor your memory and pay my respects for the first time, I found myself overwhelmed with sadness and gratitude. It was as if God's miracles and grace were the unseen threads weaving together this profound and heartfelt experience.

Thoughts of you fill my days, and sometimes, I grant myself the freedom to dream of how different my life might have been with you still by my side. The truth is, I would give anything to have you here with me today. I pray that you continue to be my guardian angel, watching over me from above, smiling with the same pride and joy that adorned your face on that beautiful day at the church when you held me in your arms. I love you immensely, Dad.

With all my love,
Your Daughter, Judy

THIRTY NINE

After enduring the weight of sorrow for an entire summer, mourning the loss of my father since the day I received his death certificate, a glimmer of hope unexpectedly pierced through the darkness. Sensing my need for connection, Tracy, a dear friend, reached out and invited me to dinner. It had been far too long since we last shared a moment and little did I know that this dinner would set in motion a series of extraordinary events.

During our meal, the conversation meandered into an unexpected turn when I delved into the topic of her father—someone I had joyfully encountered and interacted with during various family gatherings. Gratitude and warmth filled my heart as I reminisced about the caring nature of him and his wife. To my surprise, she revealed that her father had recently returned from Mexico. A spark ignited within me, prompting me to ask about the specific state. When she mentioned "Capilla," an instinct guided me to inquire further, "Capilla de Guadalupe?" Her affirmative response sent a surge of excitement through both of us.

In mere seconds, a text to her father confirmed the improbable connection. "Yes, why do you ask?" he replied. The next day, a phone call connected me with a newfound cousin, Karina, and the realization that I may have found my father's family. Emotions overwhelmed us as I shared photos of my father and me at my baptism, and my cousin Karina confirmed, "Yes, that is my tío Manuel."

In the days that followed, I grappled with the shock of this newfound reality. Years of futile attempts to locate my father's family finally come to fruition. Months of communication ensued, revealing details about my father's date of death. As the anniversary approached, I asked Karina for a heartfelt favor—to place flowers at his resting place on my behalf. She not only agreed but also sent photos and a video, allowing me a virtual connection to my father's final resting place.

Observing the lack of a tombstone, I asked another favor of Karina—to assist me in memorializing my father properly. Without hesitation, she supported my request, guiding me through the process of designing and ordering a tombstone. The joy that filled my heart upon seeing his resting place adorned with a beautiful marker featuring his photo was immeasurable.

The day of departure arrived, and as my family and I headed to the airport, emotions swirled within me. Excitement, nervousness, and anticipation filled my heart as we embarked on a trip to the quaint town of Capilla de Guadalupe. Three hours later, we landed in Guadalajara, where my cousin's husband waited to drive us to Capilla. The journey felt lengthy, but my eagerness grew with each passing mile.

After dedicating months to exploring Google Maps and studying photos, a vivid image of my father's hometown took shape in my mind. As I closed my eyes, I allowed myself to envision the sights and sounds I yearned to encounter. The anticipation grew as I imagined feeling the cool breeze on my face, and the words 'Ya llegamos a Capilla' resonated in my thoughts. The realization that I would soon be treading the same streets my father had once walked filled me with eager anticipation.

Our arrival in Capilla exceeded every dream. The narrow streets connecting our hotel to the main plaza led us to the heart of the town, where the Parroquia De Nuestra Señora de Guadalupe stood proudly. Its façade, adorned with intricate details and vibrant hues, told a story of centuries past. Surrounded by elderly citizens on iron benches, the plaza buzzed with life.

My children, excited to explore, led us across the street to Paletas "El Feo." The famous paletas were a delightful treat, and as we savored them on an iron bench in the plaza, I absorbed every second of the experience. An emotional blend of joy, sadness, loss, gratitude, and love overwhelmed me. As I closed my eyes, the sun's warmth caressed my face, instantly transporting me to an afternoon when my father, in his childhood, strolled those very streets alongside his mother.

In a serendipitous moment, a mother and her son hurried past me, and as our eyes met, a gentle smile adorned the boy's face. Overwhelmed by emotion, a tear traced its path down my cheek, a tender sign from my father in heaven, softly whispering, "Welcome home, hija." The journey to find my roots had led me to a place where I felt an undeniable connection, and in that moment, the realization dawned upon me—I had unmistakably found my way home.

The ensuing days overflowed with an abundance of love and joy. My heart expanded like never before, brimming with an overwhelming sense of happiness. Each day unfolded as a new adventure, taking me to the homes of my uncles and aunt for the very first time. Excitement and nerves mingled within me, uncertain of what to expect. Countless questions and thoughts raced through my mind, mindful of the need to respect their process, as many were unaware that my father had a daughter back in California.

To my relief, everyone welcomed my family and me with open arms. Warm embraces marked this reunion, offering a special warmth that made every visit unforgettable. Graced with hugs and welcomed into their homes, I relished the chance to meet my uncles, my only living aunt, their spouses, children, and grandchildren. The tales about my father filled the air—stories of his love, cherished by the people in their pueblo, eagerly awaiting his arrival in his blue van.

The day after my arrival and initial family meetings, I approached my cousin Karina with a request to visit my father at the cemetery. Early the next morning, I found a beautiful basket of red roses, white lilies, white daisies, and a touch of baby's breath, a thoughtful gesture from my cousin. Holding the basket on my lap, I took deep breaths during the ride, anticipating the indescribable emotions that awaited me at the cemetery.

Upon our arrival, we greeted an older man responsible for the cemetery's upkeep. Guided by my cousin, we walked towards a peach-colored chapel at the back end of the cemetery. With a gentle gesture, she pointed to the ground where my father rested. Tears welled up in my eyes as I leaned down to place the flowers at the base of the chapel. Once again, a floodgate of emotions opened, releasing the sorrow that lingered within me.

Sitting beside my father's grave, I poured out my heart, expressing love, gratitude, and the profound emptiness that had lingered within me for years. I recounted the moments of meeting his siblings, conveying thanks for the gift of life and the profound experience of being present with him. As I stayed near the peach-colored chapel, the sun's warmth enveloped me, and I found myself captivated by its beauty, allowing its miraculous embrace to permeate every fiber of my being. In the serene stillness of that moment, I felt a profound connection with my father's spirit. The vibrant flowers, symbols of life's fleeting splendor, adorned his resting place, reflecting the resilience of the human heart. Amidst the tapestry of loss and self-discovery, I found closure in healing the wounds left by my father's absence, while also cherishing the rare and precious gift of life's miracles—a poignant testament to the enduring power of love that knows no bounds of time or space.

FORTY

One year later, our family made the decision to travel to Mexico and spend Christmas with my Serratos family. The passing of my father's last remaining sister intensified my longing to spend more time with my uncles, who felt like the closest semblance to having my father by my side. Urging my husband and coordinating with my cousin Karina, plans were set in motion for a family posada—a Christmas celebration and reunion with mi familia Serratos.

To me, it felt like celebrating the first Christmas with my father that we never had the opportunity to do. My cousin took the lead in organizing the posada of the familia Serratos. She listened attentively to my vision, and, together, we worked on the intricate details to make this the most special family reunion.

This Christmas season was more than just a simple celebration for me, it was a deep emotional journey shared with my Serratos family in Mexico. Celebrating and embracing the Christmas spirit in Capilla de Guadalupe was the most beautiful and moving experience.

The essence of family, peace, and joy permeated every moment, filling my heart with overwhelming happiness. We immersed ourselves in the beautiful traditions of Mexico: the delicious food, vibrant decorations, and music.

However, the most touching part of our journey in Mexico was the time spent with my uncles and their families. I seized every opportunity to express my love, embracing each uncle with a warm hug and a tender kiss on the cheek. In those moments, I felt my father's presence around us, and I felt the need to shower them with love and affection. I truly wanted to make them feel special with the love and care that I couldn't share with my own dad.

I am deeply grateful to God and my faith for this miraculous opportunity, for revealing a true miracle in my life. Meeting and spending time with my family of origin was touching, creating memories that will be engraved in my heart forever.

A particularly moving moment occurred on my last day in Mexico when I attended mass and visited the cemetery to honor my father's resting place, adorning it with flowers. While there, my only hope was to have made him proud and that seeing his family reunited would bring a smile to him in heaven.

Amidst these cherished moments, I have come to realize that family is not just a word, it is a feeling, an emotion that binds us across time and space. This Christmas was a testament to the power of love, family, and miracles that can happen when our hearts are open.

Epilogue

In the quiet moments of reflection, I find myself humbled by the profound interconnectedness of life's delicate threads. Each moment, no matter how seemingly insignificant, carries within it the possibility for something extraordinary. Through every twist of fate, every rise and fall of life's circumstances, I've come to understand that my journey is a symphony of experiences, each note blending into the next to form a melody uniquely my own.

As I close this chapter of my memoir, I am overwhelmed with a sense of reverence for the tapestry of moments that have shaped me. Every triumph, every heartache, has left its mark upon my soul, imbuing me with a wisdom born of both joy and sorrow. With each turn of the page, I am reminded of the resilience of the human spirit, the capacity for inner strength that resides within us all.

With a heart full of gratitude, I step forward into the unknown, embracing the path that lies ahead for I know now that every step I take is a testament to the strength of love, and the guiding force that has illuminated my path even in the darkest corners of my journey. So, with reverence and hope, I bid farewell to these pages, carrying with me the lessons learned and the wisdom gained as I continue to write the story of my life.

Judy Stella

Acknowledgements

To every person who has graced the pages of my story, you are my earthly angels. Your love and kindness have touched my soul in ways words cannot express. It is because of you that I am filled with an indescribable feeling of gratitude each and every day.

To my beloved family, I am filled with boundless gratitude. My husband, your presence has been instrumental in my healing and growth. Your patience and love are unmatched, and I am deeply grateful for you. To our cherished children, Natalia and Lorenzo, you both inspire me endlessly. Natalia, your spirited nature and determination fill me with hope for a brighter future. Lorenzo, your kindness and gentle spirit remind me of the goodness in the world. Thank you for being my constant cheerleaders as I embarked on this journey of writing. I hope to make you proud.

To my mother and siblings, we have weathered storms together, and I am filled with pride for our resilience. Today, we stand united, supporting each other on our journey of healing. Know that my love for you knows no bounds.

To my dear friends, you are the stars that have illuminated my path, guiding me through life's highs and lows. From childhood to the present, you have stood by my side, offering me your unwavering love, support, and encouragement. Though too numerous to name individually, you know who you are, and I am forever grateful for your presence in my life.

Gratitude overflows from my heart to Dr. Farhat Chaudhry, my mental health therapist for the past seven years. Your compassionate guidance and unwavering support have been instrumental in my healing journey. I am eternally thankful for your wisdom, unconditional love, and acceptance.

To the teachers and counselors who have shaped my mind and nurtured my spirit, your impact is immeasurable. From my earliest days in elementary school to the present, you have been beacons of knowledge and sources of inspiration. Each of you holds a special place in my heart, and I am forever indebted to your dedication.

To the authors and mentors whose words have touched my soul, thank you for sharing your wisdom and insights with the world. Your contributions have enriched my life beyond measure, and I carry your teachings with me always.

Among the numerous books that have adorned my shelves throughout the years, and the countless authors whose writings have profoundly impacted my being, one figure stands out to whom I owe a debt of gratitude: Dr. John C. Maxwell. From the moment I discovered your work, you became like a surrogate father to me. Your books, podcasts, and messages filled my mind, heart, and soul with the invaluable life lessons, teachings, and wisdom that I yearned for, akin to what I might have received from my own father.

I'll always remember the momentous occasion when I traveled to Florida for my very first International Maxwell Conference. As I stood in line, eagerly anticipating my chance to meet you and have my book signed, I placed a Post-it bearing a special Bible scripture, Psalm 145:3, alongside it. When you noticed it, your eyes sparkled with acknowledgment, and you called out my name with enthusiasm. Meeting my gaze, warmth and tenderness radiated from your eyes, and you spoke a simple yet profound word: "Beautiful." In that instant, I felt embraced by the love and encouragement you imparted upon me. It's a memory I will cherish forever.

Thank you, Papa John, for your unwavering love, guidance, and encouragement. You've touched my life in ways you may never fully comprehend, and I am eternally grateful for the light you've brought into this world.

I also want to extend a special acknowledgement to artist Carla Morrison. Carla, your latest album "El Renacimiento" is a masterpiece. Each song resonated deeply with a different season of my life, and listening to it became a ritual as I wrote my book. Whenever I sat down to write, I'd slip on my headphones and press play on your album. And when I needed an extra dose of motivation, I'd hit repeat on "Soñar" and remind myself that this was me working on making my next dream come true. Every chapter I wrote brought me one step closer to realizing my dreams, and your music was the soundtrack to that journey.

A heartfelt thank you to Davina and Alegria Publishing whose guidance and support were invaluable as I navigated the journey of writing my first book. Your encouragement has meant the world to me. I am grateful to your team for making one of my dreams come true.

I extend my sincerest gratitude to you, dear reader, for choosing to embark on this journey with me through my book. I am filled with immense gratitude and humility. Thanks to your support, a portion of the proceeds will serve Lennox, the community where I grew up by assisting the children and families there. Your contribution is making a tangible difference in their lives, and for that, I am truly thankful.

Judy Stella

About the Author

Judy Stella is a Licensed Clinical Social Worker (LCSW) with extensive experience dedicated to supporting children and families. Her commitment to helping and empowering others stems from her personal journey of overcoming adversities during her childhood and early adulthood.

She earned her Master's degree in Social Work from the University of Southern California and her undergraduate degree in Social Work with a minor in Criminal Justice from Cal State University, Long Beach. Her educational achievements stand as a testament to her perseverance and serve as inspiration for young women pursuing higher education. A Maxwell Leadership Certified Trainer and Coach, Judy channels her passion into adding value to people's lives and helping them realize their potential.

Currently serving as the Vice President of Human Capital at Stella Health Insurance Agency, Judy draws upon her extensive background in social work to enhance the organization's mission. Demonstrating an unwavering dedication to nurturing a positive and inclusive workplace culture, she leads initiatives to foster collaboration and empowerment among all team members. Judy's strategic approach extends to talent acquisition, ensuring that recruitment efforts align closely with the agency's overarching objectives to promote sustainable growth and excellence.

Judy is a devoted mother to two small children and resides with her husband in Manhattan Beach, CA.

Let's Stay Connected

As you turn the last page of *Reverence: Echoes of Healing and Gratitude*, I hope you carry with you the stories and lessons that have shaped my journey. Your support means the world to me, and I would love to stay connected with you as we continue this path of personal growth, healing, and community together.

To receive updates on future events, special projects, and insights from my personal library—where I've discovered so many catalysts for change—please subscribe to my email list. You can also visit my website at www.judystella.com to explore my book recommendations and find inspiration for your own journey.

If you're interested in inviting me to speak at an event or conference, please reach out to my team at info@judystella.com.

Thank you for being a part of this community. Together, let's continue to embrace the power of resilience and gratitude.

With warmth and appreciation,

Mailing Address:

Judy Stella
P.O. Box 939
Manhattan Beach, CA 90267